GREAT SHORT GAMES
OF THE CHESS MASTERS

Fred Reinfeld

DOVER PUBLICATIONS, INC.
MINEOLA, NEW YORK

Published in Canada by General Publishing Company, Ltd., 30 Lesmill Road, Don Mills, Toronto, Ontario.
Published in the United Kingdom by Constable and Company, Ltd., 3 The Lanchesters, 162–164 Fulham Palace Road, London W6 9ER.

Bibliographical Note

This Dover edition, first published in 1996, is an unabridged republication of the work originally published by Collier Books, New York, in 1961.

Library of Congress Cataloging-in-Publication Data

Reinfeld, Fred, 1910–1964.
    Great short games of the chess masters / Fred Reinfeld.
        p.   cm.
    Originally published: New York : Collier Books, 1961.
    ISBN 0-486-29266-5 (pbk.)
    1. Chess—Collections of games.   I. Title.
GV1452.R357   1996
794.1'5—dc20
                                     96-22567
                                       CIP

Manufactured in the United States of America
Dover Publications, Inc., 31 East 2nd Street, Mineola, N.Y. 11501

Before You Begin

PERHAPS YOU ALREADY KNOW the elements of chess. If so, fine. If not, here's a quick summary of what you need to know about the game.

The game is played on a chessboard, with eight horizontal rows and eight vertical rows of eight squares each. All 64 squares are used.

Each player has 16 chessmen: one King, one Queen, two Rooks (or Castles), two Bishops, two Knights, and eight Pawns.

To see how these forces are placed, refer to the diagram on page v. At the beginning of the game, the King is placed on K1. The Queen is placed on Q1. The Bishops are placed on KB1 and QB1. The Knights are placed on KN1 and QN1. The Rooks are placed on KR1 and QR1.

All the chessmen mentioned thus far go on the horizontal row nearest the player. The Pawns go on the next horizontal row—at KR2, KN2, KB2, K2, Q2, QB2, QN2, and QR2. When you are all through setting up the pieces, this is the position you will have for starting the game:

Here is how the various chessmen move:

The King can move in any direction, one square at a time.

The Queen can move vertically, horizontally, and diagonally along the whole length of any line available to her. Friendly pieces may block her path, while enemy pieces on these lines can be captured by her.

The Rook can move horizontally and vertically—but only one direction at a time.

The Bishop moves diagonally, one direction at a time.

The Knight is the only piece that can leap over any other units. Its move is always of the same length: it moves one square up or down, and then two squares to the right or left or one square to the right or left, and then two squares up or down. It can capture hostile pieces only at the terminal square of its move.

The King, Queen, Rook, Bishop, and Knight all capture the way they move.

The Pawn has some curious properties. It can only move forward, one square at a time. The first time it moves, it can advance two squares. In capturing, however, it captures diagonally forward on an adjoining square.

The most important power of the Pawn is that when it reaches the last row, you can promote it to a new Queen, Rook, Bishop, or Knight. In almost all cases the new piece is a Queen—for this is the strongest of all the pieces.

Basically, the way to win a game of chess is to attack the hostile King in such a way that no matter what your opponent does, he cannot escape capture.

When the King is attacked, he is said to be in check. If he can get out of check, the game goes on. If he cannot get out of check, the King is checkmated, and the game is over.

A prospective loser does not always wait for checkmate. If he has lost too much material, he knows checkmate is inevitable, and so he resigns. If on the other hand there is not enough material to force checkmate, the game is given up as a draw, with honors even.

Here are a few more rules you need to know: White always moves first, and the board is so placed that the nearest corner square at his right is a white square. In order to get the King into a safe position, it is advisable to "castle." This is possible on the King-side when there are no pieces between the King and King Rook. Move the King next to the Rook, and then place the Rook on the other side of the King. It is also possible to castle with the Queen Rook when there are no pieces between the King and the Queen Rook. In that case, the King moves to QB1, and the Queen Rook goes to Q1.

To derive the maximum value of this book, there are two features that you will very likely want to review quickly. One is to check up on the relative values of the chessmen. Expressed in points, their values are as follows:

Queen	9 points
Rook	5 points
Bishop	3 points
Knight	3 points
Pawn	1 point

It is important to be absolutely certain of these values, for most games are decided by superiority in force.

Bishops (3 points) and Knights (3 points) are equal in value, but experienced players try to capture a Bishop in return for a Knight.

A Bishop or Knight (3 points) is worth about three Pawns (3 points). If you give up a Knight and get three Pawns in return, you may consider it as more or less an even exchange. If you lose a Knight (3 points) for only a Pawn (1 point), you have lost material and should lose the game, if you are playing against an expert.

If you capture a Rook (5 points) for a Bishop or Knight (3 points), you are said to have "won the Exchange." If you lose a Rook (5 points) for a Bishop or Knight (3 points), you have "lost the Exchange."

The other important feature in reading a chess book is to be familiar with chess notation. If you can count up to 8, this presents no problem. You may have heard scare stories to the effect that chess notation is inordinately difficult. The difficulty of chess notation is a myth, circulated by people too lazy to discover how simple and logical it really is.

The following diagram shows you all you need to know about chess notation:

BLACK

QR8	QN7	QB8	Q7	K8	KB7	KN8	KR7
QR6	QN5	QB6	Q5	K6	KB5	KN6	KR5
QR4	QN3	QB4	Q3	K4	KB3	KN4	KR3
QR2	QN1	QB2	Q1	K2	KB1	KN2	KR1

WHITE

As you see, the squares are *numbered* from both sides of the board; White's KR1, for example, is Black's KR8. Each square is also *named* for the piece occupying the file.

I honestly believe that *ten minutes' study* of this board is all you need to enable you to play over the games and examples in this book.* Although the compact treatment of games and examples makes only slight demands on your knowledge of chess notation, I should like to advise you to master the notation thoroughly; it will open the gates to a lifetime of reading pleasure.

The following are the chief abbreviations used in the chess notation:

---

* If you feel that you need more schooling in learning the notation, almost any primer will be of help. *First Book of Chess* (Sterling Publishing Company: New York, 1952) by Horowitz and Reinfeld, contains an unusually detailed treatment of chess notation.

King — K

Queen — Q

Rook — R

Bishop — B

Knight — Kt

Pawn — P

captures — ×

to — —

check — ch

discovered check — dis ch

double check — dbl ch

en passant — e.p.

castles, king-side — O–O

castles, queen-side — O–O–O

good move — !

very good move — !!

outstanding move — !!!

bad move — ?

Here are some examples of abbreviation: N–KB3 means "Knight moves to King Bishop three." Q×B means "Queen takes Bishop." R–K8 ch means "Rook moves to King eight giving check."

Contents

GREAT SHORT GAMES
OF THE CHESS MASTERS

Discredited Opening

WHITE'S SECOND MOVE has long been discredited because it leads to a loss of time when White's Queen is attacked. Add this error of commission to one or two of omission, and the result is a dazzling brilliancy.

CENTER GAME

Hastings, 1894

White	*Black*
ALLIES	BLACKBURNE
1 P–K4	P–K4
2 P–Q4	P×P
3 Q×P	N–QB3
4 Q–K3	P–KN3
5 B–Q2	. . . .

Not a bad move, if White follows up with 6 B–B3 to neutralize Black's Bishop on the long diagonal—but he doesn't.

5	B–N2
6 N–QB3	KN–K2
7 Castles	Castles
8 P–B4?	. . . .

Altogether inferior to 8 N–Q5 with a view to B–B3 and good chances of equalizing.

8	P–Q4!

Black (threatening . . . P–Q5) seizes the initiative with this move.

9 P×P	N–N5!
10 B–B4	B–B4!

Every move a threat.

11	**B—N3**	KN×P
12	**N×N**	N×N
13	**Q—KB3**	Q—B3!

Another threat—this time . . . Q×NP mate.

| 14 | **P—B3** | N—N5! |

Now Black threatens . . . N—Q6ch followed by . . . N—K4 dis ch—or . . . N—K8 dis ch)—winning White's Queen.

| 15 | **B—B4** | . . . . |

Position after 15 B—B4

| 15 | . . . . | Q—R3!! |

With this exquisite point: if White captures the Queen, Black replies 16 . . . N×P mate.

| 16 | **P—N4** | . . . . |

This feeble attempt to confuse the issue leaves Black unruffled.

| 16 | . . . . | Q×P!! |

Once more, if White replies 17 B×Q, Black has 17 . . . N×B mate. Meanwhile Black is threatening . . . Q—R8 mate or . . . Q—N8 mate, so White makes room for his King.

| 17 | **B—K3** | B×BP!! |

White resigns, as he is overwhelmed by the threats of
18 . . . Q–R8 mate or 18 . . . Q×P mate or 18 . . .
Q–N8 mate. And of course the reply to 18 QNP×B is
18 . . . Q–B7 mate.

Black has played with heart-stirring brio.

Helping Along the Good Work

BLACK'S JOB in this game seems to be helping his opponent find brilliancies. And White is most obliging.

DANISH GAMBIT

Kaschau, 1893

White	*Black*
CHAROUSEK	WOLLNER
1 P—K4	P—K4
2 P—Q4	P×P
3 P—QB3	P×P
4 B—QB4	N—KB3

Black can also capture the third Pawn, taking up a solid defensive position after 5 B×NP with 5 . . . P—QB3; 6 N—KB3, P—Q3; 7 Castles, N—Q2 followed by . . . N—B4.

5 N—B3	B—B4
6 N×P	P—Q3
7 Castles	Castles
8 N—KN5	. . . .

White has good play for the sacrificed Pawn, but it is questionable whether he would have enough after the indicated developing move 8 . . . N—B3—which, by the way, would have prevented the attack that follows.

8	P—KR3?

Driving White to do what he wants to do anyway.

9 N×P!	R×N
10 P—K5	. . . .

This is possible because the Queen Pawn is pinned. (This explains why 8 . . . N–B3 was in order.)

10	N–N5

After 10 . . . N–K1; 11 B–K3!, B–N3; 12 Q–R5, Q–K2; 13 B×B, RP×B; 14 QR–K1 White has a winning attack.

11 P–K6!	. . . .

A crushing stroke which simultaneously attacks Black's King Rook and King Knight.

Position after 11 P–K6!

BLACK

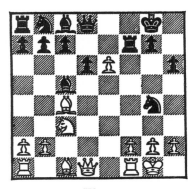

WHITE

Black has no really good move. If he plays 11 . . . R×P?! there follows 12 P–K7 dis ch, R–B2 dis ch; 13 K–R1 and White must win. Of course 11 . . . R–K2 is futile because of 12 Q×N.

Finally, after 11 . . . QB×P; 12 B×B White wins easily.

11	Q–R5!?
12 P×Rch	K–B1
13 B–B4!	N×BP
14 Q–K2	N–N5 dis ch
15 K–R1	. . . .

White threatens Q–K8 mate.

15	B–Q2
16 QR–K1!	. . . .

With a subtle threat against which Black is powerless.

16	N–QB3
17 Q–K8ch!	R×Q
18 P×R/Qch	B×Q
19 B×QP mate	

A very delightful finish. Black's inept defense has been artistically refuted.

Deceptive Simplicity

THERE IS AN ART to evolving complications from apparently colorless positions. Spielmann was a great master of this attractive art.

BISHOP'S OPENING

Ostend, 1906

White SPIELMANN	Black REGGIO
1 P–K4	P–K4
2 B–B4	N–KB3
3 P–Q3	B–B4
4 N–QB3	P–Q3
5 P–B4	N–N5

These premature fishing expeditions always come to a bad end.

6 P–B5	Q–R5ch
7 P–KN3	Q–R4
8 P–KR3!	B×N

As 8 . . . N–KB3; 9 Q×Q, N×Q; 10 KN–K2 does not look inviting, Black selects a different course.

9 Q×N	Q×Q
10 P×Q	B–N3
11 P–N5!	. . . .

Suddenly a terrific threat looms up: 12 P–N6! Spielmann knows how to put the open file to good use.

11	N–B3
12 P–N6!	BP×P
13 P×P	P–KR3

27

BLACK

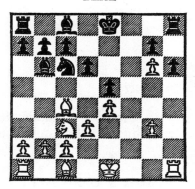

WHITE

At this point Black may have been congratulating himself on escaping with a whole skin—until he saw White's next move:

| 14 R×P‼ | R×R |

But not 14 . . . P×R; 15 P–N7, R–B1; 16 B×P and Black is lost.

| 15 B×R | . . . . |

And now 15 . . . P×B is answered by 16 P–N7, N–K2; 17 N–Q5!, B–K3 (note that 17 . . . N–N1 is refuted by the same reply); 18 N×B and White wins.

15	N–K2
16 B–B7ch	K–B1
17 B–N5	B–N5
18 K–Q2!	. . . .

Threatening instant destruction with R–R1 followed by R–R8ch etc.

| 18 . . . . | B–KR4 |

After this, 19 R–R1 still wins the Exchange, but White wants a quicker decision.

| 19 R–KB1! | . . . . |

Now Black cannot play . . . N×P or . . . B×P, as White simply recaptures with discovered check.

19	P–B3
20 P–KN4!	Resigns

Black's attacked Bishop must capture a Pawn, allowing the recapture with discovered check. Spielmann's forceful and economical attack has led to enchanting play.

Interesting Switch

SOME BANKERS have tried their hand at chess, but only one chessplayer became a banker and then a baron. This was Ignatz Kolisch, one of the brightest stars of the Romantic Era until he turned his powers of concentration to the stock market.

VIENNA GAME

(in effect)

Paris, 1859

White	Black
MANDOLFO	KOLISCH
1 P–K4	P–K4
2 B–B4	N–KB3
3 N–QB3	P–B3

Moderns prefer 3 . . . N–B3 here—or even the more complicated 3 . . . N×P.

| 4 P–Q3 | P–QN4 |

This inferior move turns out well, but 4 . . . P–Q4 is decidedly preferable.

5 B–N3	P–QR4
6 P–QR4	P–N5
7 N–R2?	. . . .

The Knight is stranded in this blind alley for the rest of the game.

7	P–Q4
8 P×P	P×P
9 N–KB3	N–B3
10 Q–K2	B–N5

Black's imposing center is under some pressure.

11 Castles	B–QB4
12 B–N5	P–R3
13 P–R3	. . . .

Very peculiar, as Black can now win the Exchange with
13 . . . B×N; 14 B×N, B×Q; 15 B×Q, B×R. But
Kolisch prefers a sublime swindle.

13	P–R4?!
14 P×B?	P×P

The open King Rook file is of course what Black was
aiming for.

15 N×KP	N–Q5
16 Q–K1	. . . .

White is a piece ahead and has the frightful threat of
N–B6 dis ch winning Black's Queen.

Position after 16 Q–K1

BLACK

WHITE

16	N–K5!!

A superb resource.

17 B×Q	N–N6!!

Threatens 18 . . . R–R8 mate.

18 N–B6 dis ch	. . . .

White sees that 18 P×N will not do because of 18 . . .
N–B6ch or 18 . . . N–K7ch—double check and mate!

18	N/Q5–K7ch
19 Q×Nch	N×Q mate

An engaging example of Kolisch's scintillating style.

All's Well That Ends Well

How THE LONE WHITE KING, unassisted by his indifferent colleagues, manages to escape from a sea of troubles, makes an exciting saga. There is no other game quite like it.

VIENNA GAME

Vienna, 1872

White	Black
HAMPPE	MEITNER
1 P–K4	P–K4
2 N–QB3	B–B4
3 N–QR4?!	. . . .

This second move of the Knight, dubious on general principles, meets with an astonishing reply.

3	B×Pch!?
4 K×B	Q–R5ch
5 K–K3	. . . .

White has little choice, for if 5 P–KN3, Q×KP and Black's Queen is attacking two pieces.

5	Q–B5ch
6 K–Q3	P–Q4
7 K–B3	Q×KP

With two Pawns for the piece and a lasting attack, Black has done well with his speculation.

8 K–N3	N–QR3

Black threatens . . . Q–QN5 mate.

White cannot very well play 9 B × N, for after 9 . . .
P × N Black will be threatening . . . R–N1ch.

    9 P–QR3   . . . .

Though White has parried the mate, he unwittingly runs
into a fantastic reply.

Position after 9 P–QR3

BLACK

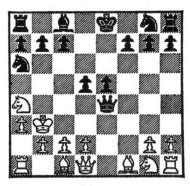

WHITE

9 . . . .   Q × Nch!!

After this amazing sacrifice—and the best is yet to come
—White will have great trouble in avoiding disaster.

    10 K × Q   N–B4ch
    11 K–N4   P–QR4ch!!
    12 K × N   N–K2

With the weird threat of 13 . . . P–QN3ch; 14 K–
N5, B–Q2 mate!

    13 B–N5ch!   K–Q1
    14 B–B6!   P–QN3ch!
    15 K–N5   N × B

With the sly threat of 16 . . . N–Q5ch; 17 K–R4,
B–Q2 mate.

Nor will 16 P–Q4 save White, for then comes 16 . . .
N × Pch; 17 Q × N, B–Q2 mate!

    16 K × N   B–N2ch!!

The idea behind this beautiful move is: 17 K × B??,

K–Q2!! and White is powerless against the coming . . . KR–QN1 mate.

17	K–N5!	B–R3ch
18	K–B6!	. . . .

Avoiding this amusing pitfall: 18 K–R4??, B–B5! with 19 . . . P–QN4 mate to follow.

18	. . . .	B–N2ch!!

The game was abandoned as a draw as Black, despite his stupendous material disadvantage, cannot be deprived of a perpetual check.

Not the Same

THERE IS an old Latin proverb to the effect that when two people do the same thing, it is not the same. In this case both players violate opening protocol by playing out the Queen early in the game. In one case this is good; in the other, bad.

VIENNA GAME

Los Angeles, 1940

(Simultaneous Exhibition)

White	*Black*
HOROWITZ	AMATEUR
1 P–K4	P–K4
2 N–QB3	N–QB3
3 B–B4	B–B4
4 Q–N4!?	....

This is best answered by 4 . . . K–B1 (despite the loss of time involved), with the threat of winning a piece by . . . P–Q4.

4	Q–B3?
5 N–Q5!	....

Forcing Black's reply, since he cannot save his Queen and simultaneously guard his King Knight Pawn and Queen Bishop Pawn.

5	Q×Pch
6 K–Q1	....

White will soon be ready for devastating pressure along the King Bishop file.

6	K–B1
7 N–R3	Q–Q5

35

Black's Queen will be out of action for the rest of the game.

| 8 P–Q3 | B–N3 |

He must be on his guard against P–B3 winning his Queen.

| 9 R–B1 | . . . . |

Already White is threatening 10 N × B and 11 R × Pch with a won game.

| 9 . . . . | N–B3 |
| 10 R × N! | . . . . |

For if 10 . . . P × R; 11 B–R6ch, K–K1; 12 Q–N7 and White wins.

| 10 . . . . | P–Q3 |

Much too late.

Position after 10 . . . P–Q3

BLACK

WHITE

11 Q × Pch!!	K × Q
12 B–KR6ch	K–N1
13 R–N6ch!!	. . . .

Prettier than 13 N–K7ch, N × N; 14 B × P mate.

| 13 . . . . | RP × R |
| 14 N–B6 mate | |

Black crippled himself by putting his Queen out of play.

Queen Odds

IT STANDS TO REASON that we cannot expect analytical perfection in a game at Queen odds. We do have a right to expect a sprightly finish, and in this case we are well rewarded.

KING'S BISHOP GAMBIT

(Remove White's Queen)

London, 1834

White	Black
COCHRANE	AMATEUR
1 P–K4	P–K4
2 P–KB4	P×P
2 B–B4	Q–R5ch
4 K–Q1	B–B4

It is always an excellent idea, especially when receiving odds, to interpolate . . . P–Q4 in order to gain time for developing the Black Queen Bishop.

5 N–KB3	Q–Q1
6 P–Q4	B–N3
7 QB×P	. . . .

White has gained a great deal of time, but he will need more than that to win at the odds.

7	P–KB3?

A big nail in Black's coffin. He should have tried . . . P–Q4 or . . . N–K2.

8 P–K5	N–K2?
9 P×P	P×P

As a result of Black's feeble seventh move, he is unable to castle.

10 N–B3	QN–B3?

Clearly 10 . . . P–Q4 is the move (see the previous note).

11 R–K1!	B–R4?
12 N–K4!	B×R?

Black succumbs. He would have been safe after 12 . . . P–KR3 or 12 . . . P–KR4.

Position after 12 . . . B×R?

BLACK

WHITE

13 N×Pch	K–B1
14 B–KR6 mate	

Some such finish was inevitable. Here we see the gap between a master and an amateur.

What Is Truth?

Is BLACK's attacking play sound? Unsound? Who can say? It doesn't really matter, for this was obviously an offhand encounter, played by Black with great zest and verve, and it makes good sense for us to take the game in the same spirit.

KIESERITZKY GAMBIT

Vienna, 1853

White	Black
MATSCHEGO	FALKBEER
1 P–K4	P–K4
2 P–KB4	P×P
3 N–KB3	P–KN4
4 P–KR4	P–N5
5 N–K5	N–KB3

White's best course is now 6 B–B4, keeping Black occupied with the threat to his King Bishop Pawn. Instead, White plays an inconsequential developing move which allows the initiative to pass to Black.

6 N–QB3	P–Q3
7 N–B4	B–K2
8 P–Q4	N–R4

Black protects his advanced King Bishop Pawn and opens a line of attack on White's weak King Rook Pawn.

9 B–K2	B×Pch
10 K–Q2	Q–N4

Threatening to win a piece by 11 . . . P—B6 dis ch; 12 K—Q3, P × B; 13 B × Q, P × Q/Qch etc.

| 11 K—Q3 | N—QB3 |

And now Black has 12 . . . N—N5ch; 13 K—Q2, P—B6 dis ch in view.

| 12 P—R3 | B—B7! |
| 13 N—Q5 | B×P?! |

Black is carried away by his enthusiasm. Apparently he is ashamed to play the more levelheaded 13 . . . K—Q1.

| 14 N×QBPch | K—Q1 |
| 15 N—Q5? | . . . . |

He might just as well have captured the Rook, since otherwise the Knight's expedition is labeled as futile.

| 15 . . . . | P—B4! |

A powerful move, much more so than White realizes.

| 16 N×QP | P×Pch |
| 17 K—B4 | . . . . |

On 17 K×P Black can play 17 . . . R—K1ch!; 18 N×R, B—KB4 mate. Nor is this the only winning method.

But after 17 K—B4 Black announced a forced mate in nine!

Position after 17 K—B4

BLACK

WHITE

Here is the mate:

17	. . . .	Q×Nch!!
18	K×Q	N–B3ch
19	K–B4	B–K3ch
20	K–N5	P–QR3ch
21	K–R4	P–N4ch
22	N×NP	P×N dbl ch
23	K×P	R–R4ch
24	K×N	B–Q4ch
25	K–Q6	N–K1 mate

Picturesque, to say the least!

Too Much of a Good Thing

WHEN AN AMATEUR IS matched against a master, it seems a good idea for the amateur to exchange as many pieces as possible in order to rule out unpleasant complications. But this is a policy that may easily backfire, as the master is adept at extracting a winning advantage from quite simplified positions.

KING'S KNIGHT GAMBIT

Pisek, 1912

(Simultaneous Exhibition)

White	Black
DURAS	ST. JES
1 P–K4	P–K4
2 P–KB4	P×P
3 N–KB3	P–Q4
4 P×P	Q×P
5 N–B3	Q–KR4
6 P–Q4	B–KN5
7 B×P	B×N

Black is eager to exchange Queens and White readily indulges him.

| 8 Q×B | Q×Q |
| 9 P×Q | . . . . |

After making three moves, Black's Queen has disappeared from the board. This leaves White considerably ahead in time.

9	N–QB3
10 B×P	N×P
11 Castles	. . . .

Position after 11 Castles

It is not easy for Black to find a good move for his attacked Knight. Consider 11 . . . N × KBP?; 12 B–N2!, N–N4; 13 B × P and White wins a Rook.

Another possibility is 11 . . . N–QB3; 12 B–N5 (or 12 B–R3) followed by KR–K1ch and Black will find the pressure on his game intolerable.

11	N–K3?
12 B–N5ch	K–K2
13 N–Q5 mate	

Black simplified into a disaster.

A Mechanical Chess Player

THE ATTEMPT TO construct an electronic chessplayer goes back to the eighteenth century. Unlike the purely electronic chessplaying machines of our own day, the early machines were fakes. They were so small and so cunningly constructed that it seemed impossible to conceal a man in them. One of the most famous of these devices was "Mephisto," conducted for a time by a noted master named Gunsberg.

KING'S GAMBIT

London, 1879

White	*Black*
GUNSBERG	AMATEUR
1 P–K4	P–K4
2 P–KB4	P×P
3 N–KB3	B–K2

The famous Cunningham Gambit—a relic of the good old days which has been refurbished in recent times.

4 B–B4	B–R5ch

The modern move 4 . . . N–KB3! is vastly superior. White answers the Bishop check in the good old style by sacrificing a handful of Pawns.

5 P–KN3	P×P
6 Castles	P×Pch
7 K–R1	. . . .

In return for the sacrificed Pawns White has a lead in

development, open lines and attacking chances. Black must be on his guard.

7	P–Q4
8 B×P	N–KB3
9 N–B3	N×B
10 N×N	B–R6

Wins the Exchange but leads to dangerous complications.

11 N×B	B×R
12 Q–N4	. . . .

Position after 12 Q–N4

BLACK

WHITE

12	Castles

Obvious . . . and bad. Possibly 12 . . . P–KN4 might be tried here, and if 13 N–B5, P–QB3 etc.

13 N–B5	P–KN3

Forced, but it creates a serious weakness nonetheless, especially along the long diagonal.

14 N/B5–K7ch	K–R1
15 P–N3!	N–Q2
16 B–N2ch	P–KB3
17 R×B	P–B3

Of course. But White has a staggering reply.

18 Q×N!!	Q×Q
19 R×P	. . . .

45

White threatens 20 R×R mate. On 19 . . . R×R he replies 20 B×R mate.

Black's "best" chance was 19 . . . K–N2; 20 R–Q6 dis ch, K–R3; 12 R×Q leaving White with a won ending.

| 19 . . . . | P–KR4? |
| 20 R–B7 mate! | |

A remarkably interesting game. Black's inaccurate defensive play cost him the game.

The Art of Odds-Giving

IN THE GOOD OLD DAYS, when the contacts between masters and duffers were much closer, odds-giving really flourished. Giving odds successfully is an art which requires great imagination, daring and sublime faith in oneself mingled with reasonable contempt for one's opponent.

MUZIO GAMBIT

(Remove White's Queen Rook)

New York, 1859

White	*Black*
MORPHY	CONWAY
1 P–K4	P–K4
2 P–KB4	P×P
3 N–KB3	P–KN4
4 B–B4	P–N5
5 P–Q4	P×N
6 Q×P	. . . .

With a considerable advantage in material, Black can afford to return some of his booty in order to gain time for development: 6 . . . P–Q4!; 7 B × P, N–KB3 and Black should live to tell the tale.

6	B–R3?
7 Castles	N–K2
8 B×P/B4	B×B

Position after 8 . . . B × B

Notwithstanding his substantial minus in material, White sacrifices some more:

9 B×Pch!	K×B

Or 9 . . . K–B1; 10 Q × B with an easy win for White (chief threat: 11 Q–R6 mate).

10 Q×Bch	K–N2
11 Q–B6ch	K–N1
12 Q–B7 mate	

A masterly example of odds-giving.

The Romantic Muzio

NOWADAYS THE MUZIO GAMBIT IS about as dated as a doily. During the Romantic Era, however, this lively opening, involving as it does the sacrifice of a piece on the fifth move, was played frequently even against very good players. Here is an example in which Andressen, one of the very greatest attacking masters of all time, is brought to his knees in a mere 17 moves.

MUZIO GAMBIT

Breslau, 1865

White	*Black*
ZUKERTORT	ANDERSSEN
1 P–K4	P–K4
2 P–KB4	P×P
3 N–KB3	P–KN4
4 B–B4	P–N5
5 Castles	. . . .

After 5 N–K5, Q–R5ch the attack threatens to pass to Black.

5	Q–K2

Still maintaining his threat to win a piece, as he holds . . . Q–B4ch in reserve, winning White's exposed Bishop.

6 N–B3!?	. . . .

The idea behind this interesting move is apparently that after 6 . . . Q–B4ch; 7 P–Q4, Q×B; 8 N–K5, Q–K3;

9 N–Q5, K–Q1; 10 B×P White will have a fierce attack in return for the sacrificed piece.

6	. . . .	P×N
7	P–Q4	P–Q3
8	N–Q5	Q–Q2
9	Q×P	N–QB3
10	Q×P	N–Q1
11	Q–N3!	. . . .

Black's position is exceedingly difficult. The point is that White's lead in development is so great that it nullifies, at least for the time being, his material minus. Thus, after 11 . . . N–K3 there follows 12 B–KN5! with a powerful threat of 13 N–B6ch.

Position after 11 Q–N3!

BLACK

WHITE

11 . . . .   P–QB3

Though this move has been roundly condemned, Black seems to have nothing better.

12 Q×N!   R×Q

Or 12 . . . P×N; 13 Q×R, P×B; 14 B–R6, Q–K2; 15 QR–K1 and White's attack must be decisive.

13 N–B6ch   K–K2
14 N×Rch!   . . . .

A droll interpolation. Black's Queen cannot run away.

14	K–K1
15 N–B6ch	K–K2
16 N×Q	B×N
17 B–KN5ch	Resigns

Black, who is down in material and position, has nothing to live for (17 . . . K–K1; 18 B×N, R×B; 19 R×P etc.). A gem of a gambit game.

The Defense Rests

EVEN MAROCZY, that great master of defense, is baffled by the intricacies of the Muzio. The fact is we are prone to forget that the defense requires at least as much determination and energy as the attack.

MUZIO GAMBIT

Vienna, 1903

White	Black
MARSHALL	MAROCZY
1 P–K4	P–K4
2 P–KB4	P×P
3 N–KB3	P–KN4
4 B–B4	P–N5
5 N–B3	P×N
6 Q×P	P–Q4

A good idea. With a piece to the good Black can afford to give up a Pawn in order to gain time for developing.

7 N×P	P–QB3

But this is self-defeating. The position called for 7 . . . B–K3 or 7 . . . N–QB3.

8 N×P	Q–B3

Threatening . . . Q–Q5ch (winning another piece) if White castles.

9 P–B3	B–R3

Black had a better line in 9 . . . Q–R5ch; 10 P–KN3, B–N5; 11 Q–B2, Q–K2 etc.

10 P–Q4	N–K2
11 Castles	Castles

After this Black is quite lost, but it is doubtful if he could hold out in the long run. Take this plausible variation: 11 . . . N–Q2; 12 N–R5!, Q×Q; 13 R×Q, B×B; 14 N–N7ch!, K–Q1; 15 B×P! (threatens 16 N–K6 mate), N–B1; 16 R×B with a winning game for White.

Position after 11 . . . Castles

BLACK

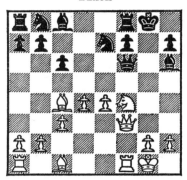

WHITE

12 N–Q5!   . . . .

A neat surprise. Black has little choice, for on 12 . . . Q×Q; 13 N×Nch regains the piece with a winning advantage. And on 12 . . . Q–Q3; 13 N–B6ch wins easily, for after 13 . . . K–N2; 14 B×Bch, K×B; 15 Q–R5ch Black is mated on the following move.

12	N×N
13 Q×Q	N×Q
14 B×B	. . . .

If Black tries 14 . . . N×P now, there follows 15 B×R, N–Q7; 16 B×Pch, K×B; 17 B–K6 dis ch, N×R; 18 R×Nch, K–K2; 19 B×B and the threat of B×P is absolutely decisive.

14	QN–Q2
15 B×R	K×B
16 P–K5	Resigns

On 16 . . . N–Q4; 17 B×N, P×B White wins more material with 18 P–K6, N–N3; 19 R×Pch etc.—not to mention his overwhelming position. This little game abounds in bright ideas.

"With All Thy Getting, Get Wisdom"

THIS IS just what Black, with his Pawn-grabbing, forgets to do. White thereby gains valuable time to build up a crushing attack.

KING'S GAMBIT DECLINED

Berlin, 1863

White	Black
NEUMANN	DUFRESNE
1 P–K4	P–K4
2 P–KB4	B–B4
3 N–KB3	P–Q3
4 B–B4	N–KB3
5 N–B3	Castles
6 P–Q3	. . . .

After 6 P×P, P×P; 7 N×P Black has an excellent reply in 7 . . . Q–Q5!

6	N–N5?

The threat of . . . N–B7 is enticing, but the simple and sound 6 . . . N–B3 was in order.

7 R–B1	N×P?

Black naively hopes for 8 N×N?, Q–R5ch followed by . . . Q×N, which would give him an excellent game.

8 R–R1!	. . . .

Now White has a splendid open King Rook file against the Black King.

8	N–N5

Again Black threatens . . . N—B7.

| 9 Q—K2 | B—B7ch? |

Waste of time. White's loss of castling doesn't signify.

10 K—B1	N—QB3
11 P—B5!	B—B4
12 N—KN5!	N—R3

Of course on 12 . . . N—B3 White wins with 13 N×
RP, N×N; 14 Q—R5 etc.

| 13 Q—R5 | Q—K1 |

White is ready to break through on the open King Rook
file.

Position after 13 . . . Q—K1

BLACK

WHITE

| 14 N×RP! | K×N |
| 15 B×N | P—KN3 |

Black sees that 15 . . . P×B will not do because of
16 Q×RPch and mate next move, while if 15 . . . P—
B3; 16 B—B1 dis ch, Q×Q; 17 R×Q mate is the answer.

| 16 Q×Pch!! | P×Q |
| 17 B×R mate | |

An artistic conclusion. White has made good use of the
open King Rook file presented to him by Black's faulty
Pawn-grabbing.

A Quiet Queen Sacrifice

THE QUEEN is so powerful that when she is sacrificed the sequel is usually violently decisive. In this case the sequel is decisive, to be sure, but there is no sign of violence. This quiet elegance gives the game a very special attraction.

FALKBEER COUNTER GAMBIT

Breslau, 1862

White	*Black*
ROSANES	ANDERSSEN
1 P–K4	P–K4
2 P–KB4	P–Q4

This countergambit surrenders a Pawn for technical and psychological reasons. The technical objective is to obtain a substantial lead in development; the psychological motive is to befuddle White.

3 KP×P	P–K5

This Pawn can be a stumbling block to White by preventing the natural N–KB3; or it can become a target for White's attack, provoking him to waste time winning the advanced Pawn.

This explains why White's best course is to shunt aside these complications and simply play 4 P–Q3, ensuring the removal of the obnoxious Pawn.

4 B–N5ch	P–QB3
5 P×P	N×P
6 N–QB3	N–KB3
7 Q–K2	. . . .

White is following the faulty tactic of winning the King Pawn. He will live to regret it.

7	**B–QB4!**
8 N×P	**Castles!**

For after 9 N×B Black wins the White Queen with 9 . . . R–K1. Or if 9 P–Q3 (since Black is threatening 9 . . . N×N; 10 Q×N, R–K1 still winning the White Queen), Black has 9 . . . N×N; 10 P×N, N–Q5 winning a piece.

9 B×N	. . . .

Getting rid of an important enemy piece, but opening up a file which will be useful to Black later on.

9	**P×B**
10 P–Q3	**R–K1**
11 B–Q2	. . . .

White prepares to castle, as the King file is getting too hot for his King.

11	**N×N**
12 P×N	**B–B4**

Developing with gain of time.

13 P–K5	**Q–N3**

A double threat: 14 . . . B×N and 14 . . . Q×P. White's reply is forced.

14 Castles	**B–Q5!**

Neat play. Black threatens mate and White cannot very well answer 15 P–QN3 because of 15 . . . Q–B4 (threatening 16 . . . Q×BP mate and also 16 . . . Q–R6ch followed by mate).

15 P–B3	**QR–N1!**
16 P–QN3	**KR–Q1!!**

A subtle move, the immediate point being 17 P×B, Q×QP and White is pathetically powerless against the coming . . . Q–R8 mate!

17 N–B3	. . . .

White can hold out longer with 17 K–N2, although after 17 . . . B–B4 he would be helpless against Black's attack. The text permits a lovely finish.

BLACK

WHITE

17 . . . .   Q×P‼

The proverbial bolt from the blue, and still threatening mate.

18 P×Q   R×P

And now, with his Queen gone, Black threatens . . . R—N8 mate.

19 B—K1   . . . .

To create a flight square for his King.

19 . . . .   B—K6ch‼
Resigns

Here we see the real point of 16 . . . KR—Q1‼ Black's devilishly posted King Rook cuts off the escape of White's King, so that Black can continue with 20 . . . R—N8 mate.

Changing Horses In Midstream

A SUDDEN CHANGE of plan can be very dangerous, especially when it involves an unmotivated alteration in one's position. Black discovers this the hard way.

PHILIDOR'S DEFENSE

Stockholm, 1937

White	Black
CASTALDI	TARTAKOVER
1 P–K4	P–K4
2 N–KB3	P–Q3

This defense is rarely played because it leads to a constricted position for Black.

3 P–Q4	N–KB3
4 N–B3	QN–Q2
5 B–K2	B–K2
6 Castles	P–KR3
7 P–QN3	. . . .

An interesting idea. The Queen Bishop is to go to Queen Knight 2, exercising indirect pressure on Black's King Pawn.

7	P–B3
8 B–N2	Q–B2

Black's only hope of salvation lies in avoiding . . . P×P, which would open up the game favorably for White.

9 Q–Q2	P–KN4

But this move, which weakens Black on the long diagonal and undermines the security of his King Knight, is of dubious value. He should have kept to his original plan of playing a tight defensive game.

<table>
<tr><td>10 KR–Q1</td><td>N–B1?</td></tr>
</table>

And this is a direct blunder. Black intends . . . N–N3–B5 but never makes it. He should at least have tried 10 . . . N–R2, in the hope of carrying out the maneuver . . . KN–B1–N3.

Position after 10 . . . N–B1?

<small>BLACK</small>

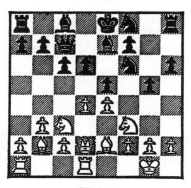

<small>WHITE</small>

<table>
<tr><td>11 P×P!</td><td>P×P</td></tr>
<tr><td>12 N×KP!</td><td>. . . .</td></tr>
</table>

The bombshell. If Black plays 12 . . . Q×N White replies 13 N–Q5! giving Black the choice between 13 . . . Q×B; 14 N–B7 mate and 13 . . . Q–Q3; 14 N×Nch and wins.

<table>
<tr><td>12 . . . .</td><td>B–K3</td></tr>
<tr><td>13 N–N5!</td><td>. . . .</td></tr>
</table>

With this pretty possibility: 13 . . . P×N; 14 B×Pch, N/B1–Q2; 15 B×Nch and Black can choose between 15 . . . B×B; 16 N×B, Q×N; 17 Q×Qch, N×Q; 18 B×R or 15 . . . K–B1; 16 B×B, P×B; 17 N–N6ch. In either case White wins the Exchange with an easy victory.

<table>
<tr><td>13 . . . .</td><td>Q–N1</td></tr>
<tr><td>14 Q–R5!</td><td>. . . .</td></tr>
</table>

One pretty move after another. If Black tries 14 . . .
P—N3 there follows 15 N×QBP, P×Q; 16 N×Q and
now 16 . . . R×N is answered by 17 N—B7 mate—or
if 16 . . . B—Q1; 17 R×Bch!, K×R; 18 B×Nch and
wins.

And of course if 14 . . . P×N; 15 B×Pch wins.

14	**B—Q1**
15 **R×Bch!**	**Q×R**
16 **N—B7ch**	**Resigns**

For if 16 . . . K—K2; 17 B—R3ch, K—Q1; 18 N×B-
dbl ch, K—K1; 19 N—N7 mate. A model of relentless exploitation of the opponent's mistakes.

The Same—But Different

ONE OF THE great charms of chess is its inexhaustibility. The double-Rook sacrifice never palls because it always appears in new guises.

PHILIDOR'S DEFENSE

Paris, 1937

White	*Black*
BERNSTEIN	TARTAKOVER
1 P–K4	P–K4
2 N–KB3	P–Q3
3 P–Q4	N–KB3
4 P×P	N×P
5 B–QB4	. . . .

White threatens to win with Q–Q5. The safest defense is 5 . . . P–QB3.

5	B–K3

Black selects a more venturesome line, which allows White to win a Pawn in very risky fashion.

6 B×B	P×B
7 Q–K2	P–Q4
8 Q–N5ch	N–QB3

There is more here than meets the eye, as in this pretty line of play: 9 Q×NP?, N–N5; 10 Q–N5ch, P–B3; 11 Q–R4, N–B4!! winning White's Queen (for if 12 Q×N, N–Q6ch).

9 N–Q4	Q–Q2
10 Q×NP?	. . . .

White cannot bypass this inviting move, especially as he

sees that 10 N×N will leave him seriously behind in development.

Position after 10 N×P

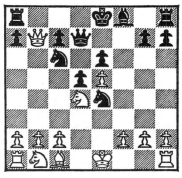

10	B–N5ch!
11 P–QB3	. . . .

Black has three pieces under attack.

| 11 . . . . | N×N!! |

Leaving White little choice, for after 12 P×B, Castles Black has too many strong threats.

12 Q×Rch	K–B2
13 Q×R	Q–N4!
Resigns	

White has no defense against the threat of . . . Q–K7 mate. White's stubborn plan to win material by a series of faulty Queen moves led to disaster.

The Austrian Morphy

WILHEM STEINITZ, famous as the man who elaborated the theory of playing for "small advantages," was so brilliant a player in his youth that he was dubbed "the Austrian Morphy." Here is the kind of game on which his reputation was based.

SCOTCH GAMBIT

Vienna, 1860

White	*Black*
REINER	STEINITZ
1 P–K4	P–K4
2 N–KB3	N–QB3
3 P–Q4	P×P
4 B–B4	B–B4
5 Castles	P–Q3
6 P–B3	B–KN5!

Stronger than 6 . . . P×P, which gives White a good initiative after 7 N×P in return for the sacrificed Pawn.

7 Q–N3	B×N

Black does not fear the coming complications.

8 B×Pch	K–B1
9 B×N	R×B
10 P×B	P–KN4!

Black hopes for an attack on the castled King.

11 Q–K6	N–K4
12 Q–B5ch	K–N2
13 K–R1	. . . .

Here 13 B×P is a mistake: 13 . . . K–R1!; 14 P–
KR4, P–KR3 and the Bishop is lost.

| 13 . . . . | K–R1 |
| 14 R–N1 | P–N5! |

Black reckons on 15 P×NP, Q–R5 with a powerful
initiative for his aggressively posted pieces.

| 15 P–KB4 | N–B6 |
| 16 R×P | . . . . |

Or 16 R–N2, N–K8; 17 R–N1, N–B7 and Black wins.

Position after 16 R×P

BLACK

WHITE

| 16 . . . . | Q–R5! |

An unpleasant surprise: if 17 R × Q, R–N8 mate.

| 17 R–N2 | Q×RPch! |

Stubborn fellow, this Steinitz.

| 18 R×Q | R–N8 mate |

A dashing win by the Austrian Morphy. White's Queen-
side pieces are still on their home squares—typical of such
games.

Presto!

A RECOGNIZED MASTER once lost his Queen on the eighth move! This is how it happened:

SCOTCH GAME

Paris, 1888

White	*Black*
FRAZER	TAUBENHAUS
1 P–K4	P–K4
2 N–KB3	N–QB3
3 P–Q4	P×P
4 N×P	Q–R5

As is made clear in the notes to many of the games in this book, early Queen moves should be avoided. Experience shows that such premature development merely exposes the Queen to attack.

5 N–QB3	N–KB3?

A developing move, to be sure, but it is risky and ill timed. The "right" way was 5 . . . B–N5 threatening . . . Q×KPch. This at least would have been consistent and would have involved relatively less risk than the actual line pursued by Black.

6 N–B5	Q–R4??

The only move to hold the game—even for the time being—was 6 . . . Q–N5.

Position after 6 . . . Q–R4??

Now White wins the Black Queen.

| 7 B–K2 | Q–N3 |
| 8 N–KR4 | Resigns |

The Black Queen is trapped! A game with a moral.

The Threat is Stronger than the Execution

WHITE'S THREAT to win a pinned piece turns out to be a "paper tiger." Black's demonstration is both neat and convincing.

SCOTCH GAME

Match, 1888

White	Black
DELMAR	LIPSCHUETZ
1 P–K4	P–K4
2 N–KB3	N–QB3
3 P–Q4	P×P
4 N×P	N–B3
5 N×N	NP×N
6 B–Q3	P–Q4

The usual course is now 7 P×P, P×P. White tries for more, achieves less.

7 P–K5	N–N5
8 Castles	. . . .

Both players realize that 8 . . . N×KP would lose a piece to 9 R–K1, B–Q3 (or 9 . . . P–B3); 10 P–KB4 etc.

8	B–QB4

A good developing move which prevents P–KB4 and rules out R–K1 for the time being.

White can now guard his King Pawn with 9 B–KB4 but in that case Black gets a sharp initiative with 9 . . . P–N4!; 10 B–N3, P–KR4! etc.

9 P–KR3	N×KP!
10 R–K1	Q–B3!

Black sets a deep trap instead of playing the lackluster 10 . . . P–B3.

11 Q–K2	**Castles!**

Naturally 11 . . . B–Q3? will not do because of 12 P–KB4 winning the Knight. But now the Knight is lost anyway.

Position after 11 . . . Castles!

BLACK

WHITE

12 Q×N	Q×Pch

This forces White's reply, since 13 K–R2 would lose White's Queen (13 . . . B–Q3).

13 K–R1	B×P!

An unexpected resource which threatens mate and forces the win of White's Queen after all.

14 P×B	Q–B6ch
15 K–R2	B–Q3
16 Q×B	Q–B7ch!

White resigns, as Black can pick up the Rook with check before confiscating the White Queen. Black displayed commendable originality in discounting the loss of his pinned Knight.

The Two-Rook Sacrifice

THIS IS one of the most spectacular themes in the whole realm of chess. It has inspired some strikingly brilliant attacks.

GIUOCO PIANO

Breslau, 1909

White	*Black*
A. LASKER	E. LASKER
1 P–K4	P–K4
2 N–KB3	N–QB3
3 B–B4	N–B3
4 P–Q3	B–B4
5 B–KN5	P–Q3
6 P–KR3	B–K3
7 B–N5	P–QR3
8 B×Nch	P×B

So far the opening has lived up its name ("quiet game"). Now it starts to liven up.

9 P–Q4	P×P
10 N×P	B×N
11 Q×B	P–B4
12 Q–B3?	. . . .

Inferior to 12 Q–K3, which would have avoided the ensuing complications.

Position after 12 Q–B3?

BLACK

WHITE

| 12 . . . . | N×P! |
| 13 Q×NP | . . . . |

The spineless alternative 13 B × Q, N × Q leaves White a Pawn down.

13	Q×B!!
14 Q×Rch	K–Q2
15 Q×R	Q–B8ch

Now we see why Black sacrificed his Rooks. He has a mating attack.

| 16 K–K2 | Q×BPch! |
| 17 K–K3 | Q×BPch! |

Black has his eye on this pretty mate: 18 K×N, B–B4ch; 19 K–Q5, Q–Q5 mate.

| 18 K–Q3 | P–B5ch |
| 19 K×N | P–KB4 mate |

A pretty finish. The rationale behind the two-Rook sacrifice is clear: the loser's Queen, in the process of confiscating the Rooks, wanders too far afield to be of any further use.

Winning Recipe

A LONG LIST of brilliant games demonstrates that when Black subjects himself to the Fried Liver Attack, his goose is likely to be cooked—if White doesn't make hash out of him.

TWO KNIGHTS' DEFENSE

(Remove White's Queen Rook)

New Orleans, 1858

White	Black
MORPHY	AMATEUR
1 P–K4	P–K4
2 N–KB3	N–QB3
3 B–B4	N–B3
4 N–N5	P–Q4
5 P×P	N×P

Risky but playable.

6 N×BP?!	. . . .

Astounding under the circumstances—White is already spotting the odds of a Rook to begin with.

6	K×N
7 Q–B3ch	K–K3

White's idea is clear: in order to protect his attacked Knight, Black's King must venture into dangerous ground.

8 N–B3	N–Q5?

Black needlessly takes chances. The alternative 8 . . . N/B3–K2 is much safer.

9 B×Nch	K–Q3
10 Q–B7	. . . .

White threatens 11 N–K4 mate. But Black can escape with a whole skin by simply playing 10 . . . Q–K2!

10	**B–K3?**
11 **B×B**	**N×B**
12 **N–K4ch**	**K–Q4**
13 **P–QB4ch!**	**K×N**

The safer-looking 13 . . . K–B3 won't do: 14 Q× Nch, B–Q3; 15 Q–Q5ch, K–Q2; 16 P–B5 with a winning game for White.

14 **Q×N**	**Q–Q5?**

After this Black is irretrievably lost. With 14 . . . K– Q5! he might have been able to hold out.

Position after 14 . . . Q–Q5?

BLACK

WHITE

15 **Q–N4ch**	**K–Q6**

Black's King is marched to his doom.

16 **Q–K2ch**	**K–B7**
17 **P–Q3 dis ch!**	**K×B**

The condemned man ate a hearty meal. However, after 17 . . . K–N8; 18 Castles, K×P; 19 Q–B2! there is nothing Black can do against the coming advance of White's Queen Knight Pawn.

18 **Castles, mate!**

This charming finish has drastically exploited Black's neglect of his most effective defensive resources.

Bishops in the Background

FEW FORCES in chess are more powerful than two smoothly cooperating Bishops trained against the hostile castled King.

FOUR KNIGHTS' GAME

Warsaw, 1917

White	*Black*
BELSITZMANN	RUBINSTEIN
1 P—K4	P—K4
2 N—KB3	N—QB3
3 N—B3	N—B3
4 B—N5	N—Q5!

Black has no intention of sticking to dull symmetry with 4 . . . B—N5 etc. In the event of 5 N × P in reply to his last move, he would continue 5 . . . Q—K2; 6 P—B4, N × B; 7 N × N, P—Q3 with a good game.

5 B—B4	B—B4
6 N×P	Q—K2!

A tricky move. If White plays 7 B × Pch he will come out a piece down after 7 . . . K—Q1. And on 7 N × BP, P—Q4!; 8 N × R, P × B Black will eventually confiscate the wayward Knight.

7 N—Q3?	. . . .

White condemns the Knight to uselessness and also blocks his Queen Pawn, hence the development of his Queen Bishop. Surely 7 N—B3 was in order.

7	P—Q4!

74

One important point of this unexpected thrust is that after 8 N × B?, P × B! White's advanced Knight would be in a bad way.

8 N×P	Q×Pch
9 N–K3	B–Q3
10 Castles	P–QN4!

In return for his sacrificed Pawn Black is achieving a magnificent development. The energetic text move prepares for . . . B–N2.

| 11 B–N3 | B–N2 |
| 12 N–K1 | Q–R5! |

By threatening . . . Q × RP mate Black forces a weakening in White's Pawn position. This enhances the long-range striking power of the Black Bishops; it also gives Black an opportunity to open a new attacking line.

| 13 P–N3 | Q–R6 |
| 14 P–QB3 | . . . . |

Position after 14 P–QB3

BLACK

WHITE

Instead of retreating his attacked Knight, Black plays:

| 14 . . . . | P–KR4! |

The coming opening of the King Rook file must be decisive.

| 15 P×N | P–R5! |

Black threatens . . . P × P with immediate disaster for White.

White can try to ward this off by setting up a defense along the second rank, but even this is doomed to failure, for example: 16 P—B3, P×P; 17 Q—K2, P×Pch; 18 K—R1, N—R4! (threatens . . . N—N6 mate); 19 N—B5 dis ch, K—B1; 20 R—B2, R—K1; 21 Q—B1, R×N!; 22 Q×R, Q×Pch! (or 22 . . . B×Pch); 23 R×Q, B×R mate.

16 Q—K2	Q×RPch!!

White resigns, for after 17 K×Q there follows 17 . . . P×P dbl ch; 18 K—N1, R—R8 mate.

Note the artful way in which Black combined the action of his Bishops with the Rook thrust along the open King Rook file.

Double or Nothing

DOUBLE ATTACK is the most potent offensive tactic in chess: one unit attacks two. To apply this technique so as to force resignation on the eighth move—that takes a bit of doing!

THREE KNIGHTS' GAME

Vienna, 1914

White	Black
RETI	DUNKELBLUM
1 P–K4	P–K4
2 N–QB3	N–QB3
3 N–B3	B–B4

Black avoids the symmetrical 3 . . . N–B3, which leads to a notoriously dull game. But disaster is too high a price to pay for novelty.

4 N×P	N×N
5 P–Q4	B×P?

Much better is 5 . . . B–Q3; 6 P×N, B×P etc.

| 6 Q×B | . . . . |

Now the attacked Knight must not move, and 6 . . . P–KB3 is not inviting. So Black chooses a different move —which proves fatal.

| 6 . . . . | Q–B3 |

Black threatens to win White's Queen with . . . N–B6ch.

Position after 6 . . . Q–B3

Black

WHITE

7 N–N5!	. . . .

A very awkward move for Black to meet.

7	K–Q1
8 Q–B5!	Resigns

White threatens 9 Q–B8 mate and also 9 Q × BPch.
There is no satisfactory way of parrying, for example 8
. . . N–N3; 9 Q × BPch, K–K2; 10 B–K3! with the
deadly threats of 11 B–B5ch or 11 B–Q4. An astonishing
conclusion.

Even as You and I

IT IS AN INSOLUBLE MYSTERY—and doubtless also a great comfort to the rest of us—that a great master can lose a game in 15 moves. What is curious about this game is that Black's position, starting with a plausible concept, simply erodes from move to move; so that Black folds up from lack of good moves.

RUY LOPEZ

Budapest, 1926

White	*Black*
YATES	RUBINSTEIN
1 P–K4	P–K4
2 N–KB3	N–QB3
3 B–N5	P–QR3
4 B–R4	N–B3
5 Q–K2	P–QN4
6 B–N3	B–B4

This development is attractive because it looks more aggressive than the customary . . . B–K2. But the move has possible drawbacks: the Bishop is exposed to attack and is likely to be out of play; worse yet, a later pin by B–KN5 may turn out to be troublesome.

7 P–B3	Q–K2
8 Castles	P–Q3
9 R–Q1	Castles
10 P–Q4	. . . .

Compare the previous note. Black's "actively" posted Bishop is really useless.

10	B–N3
11 B–N5	. . . .

Position after 11 B–N5

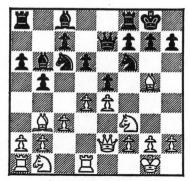

| 11 . . . . | N–Q1 |

A serious inaccuracy. The right move was 11 . . . P–R3, driving back White's pinning Bishop to King Rook 4 and thus rendering N–R4 impossible.

| 12 N–R4! | . . . . |

White pounces on his opponent's lapse. The point is that 12 . . . P–R3? would now be refuted by 13 N–N6!

| 12 . . . . | N–K3? |

Simply suicide, as White's Knight comes in with shattering power.

| 13 N–B5 | . . . . |

With this sly point: if Black plays 13 . . . Q–Q1 White replies 14 B/N3×N!, P×B; 15 N×NP!, K×N; 16 P×P and the double pin spells Black's doom.

| 13 . . . . | Q–K1 |

Black avoids the pin but not defeat.

| 14 B/N5×N | P×B |
| 15 B×N | Resigns |

Because after 15 . . . P×B; 16 Q–N4ch Black has to play 16 . . . Q–N3 to stop mate, whereupon 17 N–K7ch wins his Queen. A meaty little game.

Development Backwards

EVEN THE MASTERS sometimes indulge in the luxury of neglecting development of the pieces in the opening. One of the most pernicious forms this can take is to move an already developed piece to a less useful square. Given an alert opponent, the tragic consequences are soon all too clear.

RUY LOPEZ

Nuremberg, 1892

White	Black
TARRASCH	TAUBENHAUS
1 P–K4	P–K4
2 N–KB3	N–QB3
3 B–N5	P–QR3
4 B–R4	N–B3
5 Castles	N×P
6 P–Q4	P–QN4
7 B–N3	P–Q4
8 P×P	. . . .

So far a standard sequence, with 8 . . . B–K3 as the customary method of guarding Black's Queen Pawn.

| 8 . . . . | N–K2? |

Black wastes precious time by moving the Knight a second time; he moves it to an inferior square; and he blocks the development of his King Bishop. Thus we have here a triple blunder in a single move.

BLACK

WHITE

9	P–QR4	B–K3
10	Q–K2	P–QB3
11	P–B3	N–N3
12	N–Q4!	. . . .

By attacking Black's Queen Bishop Pawn White gains time for the powerful advance of his King Bishop Pawn, which will throw Black's forces into worse disorder.

It will not do for Black to guard the threatened Pawn with 12 . . . Q–Q2; for then comes 13 P×P, BP×P; 14 N×P!

12	. . . .	B–Q2
13	P×P	RP×P
14	R×R	Q×R
15	B–B2	. . . .

White's King Pawn is immune from capture. If 15 . . . N×KP?; 16 P–B3 wins a piece for White.

| 15 | . . . . | N–B4 |
| 16 | P–KB4! | B–K2 |

Black tries to resume his development, but it is much too late.

| 17 | P–B5! | Resigns |

Black's surrender comes as a shock, but there is good reason for it.

82

If he moves his attacked Knight to King Rook 5, White wins a piece with 18 P–KN3. On the other hand, if Black retreats his Knight (17 . . . N–B1), then White wins a piece with 18 P–B6! For example: 18 . . . B–Q1; 19 P×P—or 18 . . . P×P; 19 P×P etc.

"The Soul of the Game"

"THE PAWNS," said the great Philidor, "are the soul of the game." A weakness in Black's Pawn structure in the following game leads to the direst of consequences.

RUY LOPEZ

Southport, 1924

White	Black
ATKINS	GIBSON
1 P–K4	P–K4
2 N–KB3	N–QB3
3 B–N5	P–QR3
4 B–R4	N–B3
5 Castles	N×P

This move has the *possible* drawback of leading to a weakening of Black's Pawn structure.

6 P–Q4	P–QN4
7 B–N3	P–Q4
8 P×P	B–K3
9 P–B3	B–K2
10 B–K3	Castles
11 QN–Q2	P–B4

This move is of doubtful value because after White's reply Black's Pawn position will be in a shaky state. This is particularly true of the diagonal leading from White's King Bishop to Black's King.

12 P×P e.p.	N×P/B3
13 N–N5	B–KB4?

And this inexactitude compounds Black's difficulties. The safer course was 13 . . . Q–Q2.

84

Position after 13 . . . B—KB4?

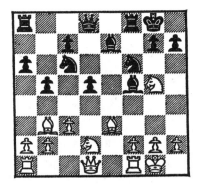

14 N/Q2—K4!! ....

This surprise move underlines Black's troubles on the weakened diagonal. Observe that his Queen Pawn is pinned.

14 .... **N×N**

Black must lose some material. For example, if he plays 14 . . . B×N White replies 15 N.×B and Black's Queen Pawn must go. In that case the reply to 15 . . . N×N would be 16 B×Pch, K—R1; 17 B×N/B6 and White wins at least the Exchange.

15 Q×Pch ....

To this Black's relatively best reply is 15 . . . Q×Q; 16 B×Qch, K—R1; but after 17 N×N White would have achieved his objective: winning the weakened Queen Pawn. Avoiding this, Black falls into something much worse.

15 .... **K—R1??**
16 Q—N8ch!! **R×Q**

Forced.

17 N—B7 mate!

One must admire the single-mindedness with which White exploited the weakness in Black's Pawn structure.

85

The Value of Surprise

IN CHESS AS IN WAR, an opponent taken by surprise is half defeated. Here is a brilliant case in point, giving us the insidious notion that third-rate surprise moves are "better" than first-rate logical moves. At any rate, this cynical concept adds to the charm of chess.

RUY LOPEZ

Munich, 1941

White	Black
RICHTER	CORTLEVER
1 P–K4	P–K4
2 N–KB3	N–QB3
3 B–N5	P–QR3
4 B–R4	N–B3
5 Castles	N×P
6 P–Q4	P–QN4

So far so good. Everything has proceeded along well-trodden paths.

| 7 P–Q5!? | . . . . |

But this comes as a complete surprise (instead of the conventional 7 B–N3), played to rattle Black.

| 7 . . . . | N–K2 |
| 8 R–K1 | N–QB4? |

But this is too much of a good thing: the Knight moves are losing too much time. With 8 . . . P–KB4 or even 8 . . . P×B Black would have had a safe game. Now White is ready for a brisk attack.

BLACK

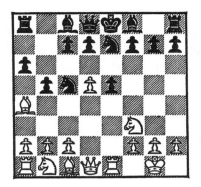

WHITE

9 N×P! ....

Black cannot capture White's Bishop because of the tricky continuation 10 Q–B3! (threatens mate), P–KB3; 11 Q–R5ch, P–N3; 12 N × NP!, P × N; 13 Q × P mate.

9 .... P–Q3

The obnoxious Knight is driven away, only to go to an even more troublesome spot.

10 N–B6 ....

Of such Knights, posted deep in the enemy's territory, it has been truly said that they are "like a rusty nail in your knee."

10 .... Q–Q2
11 B–N5! ....

White reinforces the terrible pin with diabolical energy. If Black tries 11 . . . P–B3 there follows 12 B×P!, P×B; 13 Q–R5 mate.

11 .... Q–N5
12 Q×Q B×Q

If Black thinks that the exchange of Queens will relieve the pressure, he is sadly mistaken.

13 B×N N×B

87

Or 13 . . . B×B; 14 R×Bch, K—B1; 15 B—N3 and White is a piece to the good.

| 14 B×QP dis ch! | K—Q2 |
| 15 B×B | Resigns |

Black realizes that after 15 . . . R×B White will continue 16 N—K5ch winning a piece. White's crafty policy of creating confusion in Black's ranks has paid off handsomely.

Surprise!

IN A BOOK full of Queen sacrifices, the Queen sacrifice in in this game stands out as really remarkable. In fact, the whole game is off the beaten track.

RUY LOPEZ

Antwerp, 1901

White	*Black*
FOX	AMATEUR
1 P–K4	P–K4
2 N–KB3	N–QB3
3 B–N5	N–B3
4 Castles	N×P

The old Berlin Defense, rarely seen nowadays.

| 5 R–K1 | . . . . |

The alternative 5 P–Q4 is more likely to create difficulties for Black.

| 5 . . . . | N–Q3! |
| 6 N×P | B–K2 |

Of course not 6 . . . N×B??; 7 N.×N dis ch winning Black's Queen.

7 B–B1	Castles
8 P–Q4	N–B4
9 P–QB3	P–Q4

Here Black has an easier game with 9 . . . N×N; 10 P×N, P–Q3.

10 Q–Q3	R–K1
11 P–KB4	N–Q3
12 R–K3	N–R4?

89

Feeble. Much better was . . . B—B4—K5.

| 13 N—Q2 | N—B4? |
| 14 R—R3 | N—R5? |

Instead of effectively centralizing his Queen Bishop, Black has badly posted his Knights at the sides of the board.

| 15 P—KN4 | N—N3 |
| 16 R—R5 | . . . . |

White wants to step up the pressure with Q—R3, but Black's next move offers a stunning inspiration.

| 16 . . . . | N—B3 |

Position after 16 . . . N—B3

BLACK

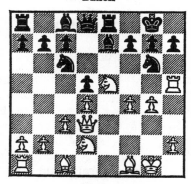

WHITE

| 17 N/Q2—B4!! | . . . . |

One of the deepest surprise moves ever played. Had Black dreamt of what was coming, he would have tried 17 . . . N/B3 × N.

| 17 . . . . | P × N |
| 18 Q × N!! | . . . . |

The expendable Queen. After 18 . . . BP × Q there follows 19 B × Pch, K—B1; 20 N × Pch, P × N; 21 R—R8 mate.

| 18 . . . . | RP × Q |
| 19 N × NP! | P × N |

White was threatening 20 R—R8 mate.

| 20 B × Pch | Resigns |

Black cannot stop mate. Truly an unconventional game.

Little Acorns

WHAT SEEMS TO BE a slight inaccuracy in the opening will often grow and grow until it assumes the proportions of a major blunder. The better a player is the quicker he will be to realize the true significance of such moves.

RUY LOPEZ

Vienna, 1911

White	Black
WOLF	HAAS
1 P–K4	P–K4
2 N–KB3	N–QB3
3 B–N5	N–B3
4 Castles	N×P
5 P–Q4	N–Q3
6 B×N	NP×B

Much better is 6 . . . QP×B!; 7 P×P, N–B4; 8 Q×Qch, K×Q. Black's King is quite safe in the center and his two Bishops vs. Bishop and Knight constitute an advantage in the ending.

7 P×P	N–N2

The unfortunate Knight never budges from this miserable retreat for the rest of the game.

8 N–B3	B–K2
9 N–Q4	Castles
10 B–K3	P–QB4

After this Black's Pawn position becomes awkward and his banished Knight cannot get back into the game via

. . . N–B4. But as matters stand, Black cannot advance his Queen Pawn until he drives off White's Knight.

11 N–B5	P–Q3
12 N×Bch	Q×N
13 N–Q5	. . . .

A powerful Knight.

| 13 . . . . | Q–Q1 |
| 14 Q–R5 | R–K1 |

Position after 14 . . . R–K1

BLACK

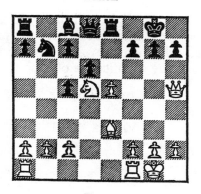

WHITE

| 15 B–N5! | . . . . |

An ingenious, well calculated Pawn sacrifice.

| 15 . . . . | R×P |

As this apparently wins a piece, White has had to calculate the sequel very exactly.

| 16 KR–K1! | . . . . |

First point: on 16 . . . R×N there follows 17 B×Q, R×Q; 18 R–K8 mate. Or 16 . . . R×B; 17 Q×R!, Q×Q; 18 R–K8 mate.

| 16 . . . . | P–KB3 |
| 17 P–KB4! | . . . . |

Second point: on 17 . . . R×N White forces mate with 18 R–K8ch etc.

| 17 . . . . | P–N3 |

At last Black seems sure of winning a piece.

18 Q–R6	R×N
19 B×P!	. . . .

Third point: on 19 . . . Q×B White forces mate with 20 R–K8ch etc.

19	Q–B1

And now comes the final point.

20 R–K8!!	Resigns

For if 20 . . . Q×R; 21 Q–N7 mate. Note Black's congested Queen-side.

Transposed Moves

TRANSPOSING MOVES—changing the order of a series of move—has lost games and won them. Here is an impressive case in point.

RUY LOPEZ

Amsterdam, 1933

(Simultaneous exhibition)

White	Black
ALEKHINE	MINDENO
1 P–K4	P–K4
2 N–KB3	N–QB3
3 B–N5	P–Q3
4 P–Q4	P×P
5 Q×P	. . . .

This gets the Queen strongly into play and prepares for Queen-side castling.

5	B–Q2
6 B×N	B×B
7 N–QB3	N–B3
8 B–N5	B–K2
9 Castles(Q)	Castles
10 P–KR4!	P–KR3

Position after 10 . . . P–KR3

| 11 N–Q5 | . . . . |

This clever sacrifice of a piece is based on White's expectation of making good use of the resulting opening of the King Rook file.

11	P×B?
12 N×Bch!	Q×N
13 P×P	N×P

After 13 . . . Q×P; 14 P×N, Q×Q; 15 R×Q the threat of R–KN4 is decisive.

| 14 R–R5 | . . . . |

White wants to double Rooks on the open file with a view to R–R8 mate. This means that Black must play up his King Bishop Pawn sooner or later in order to open an escape hatch for his King.

| 14 . . . . | Q–K3 |

After 14 . . . P–B4; 15 P–N6! (nailing down the Black King) we get the same finish as in the game.

| 15 QR–KR1 | P–KB4 |

It seems that Black is safe after all, because after 16 P–N6, Q×P; 17 Q–B4ch, he has 17 . . . P–Q4 (not 17 . . . R–B2?? or 17 . . . Q–B2??; 18 R–R8 mate).

| 16 N–K5!! | . . . . |

95

Threatens 17 R—R8 mate.

16 . . . .   P×N

Or 16 . . . Q×N; 17 Q×Q, P×Q; 18 P—N6 forcing mate.

17 P—N6!   Resigns

For Black realizes that after 17 . . . Q×P White forces mate beginning with 18 Q—B4ch. Thus we see that White's win was made possible by transposing P—N6 and N—K5. A subtle line of reasoning.

Check!

IN MANY a harmless-looking position there lurks a check
—or the possibility of a check—that spells disaster for
the opponent. White's tenth move ranks high in this category.

RUY LOPEZ

Prague, 1951

White	*Black*
FILIP	HRUSKOVA-BELSKA
1 P–K4	P–K4
2 N–KB3	N–QB3
3 B–N5	P–Q3
4 P–Q4	P×P

Black does better to hold the center for a while with 4
. . . B–Q2; 5 N–B3, N–B3 etc. As played, the White
pieces soon become unpleasantly aggressive.

5 N×P	B–Q2
6 B×N	P×B
7 N–QB3	B–K2
8 Q–B3!	B–N4?

Black's overanxious desire to simplify leads to trouble.

Position after 8 . . . B—N4?

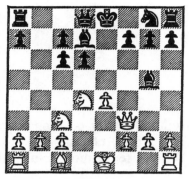

BLACK

WHITE

9 P—K5!	**. . . .**

A very difficult situation for Black, for example 9 . . . P×P; 10 N×P and White has all the play. Or 9 . . . B×B; 10 R×B, Q—N4; 11 Castles and again White has a strong initiative.

9	**P—Q4?**
10 P—K6!	**Resigns**

An amusing and amazing denouement.

White threatens 11 Q×P mate. If Black plays 10 . . . P×P then 11 Q—R5ch wins a piece. On the other hand, if Black plays 10 . . . B×P then 11 N×B, P×N; 12 Q—R5ch still wins a piece.

All this came about as a result of Black's ill-judged 8 . . . B—N4?

Obliging Opponents

REPEATEDLY WE ARE TOLD that chess is a contest, a duel,
a struggle. Yet how often does the game turn into a grace-
ful minuet in which one player bows low and offers the
game to his opponent. White's 8th move falls into this
category.

RUY LOPEZ

Berlin, 1851

White	Black
MAYET	ANDERSSEN
1 P–K4	P–K4
2 N–KB3	N–QB3
3 B–N5	B–B4
4 P–B3	N–B3
5 B×N	. . . .

The modern master, who sets more store by his Bishops,
prefers 5 P–Q4, setting up a strong Pawn center and driving off Black's annoying Bishop.

5	QP×B
6 Castles	. . . .

Premature, as will soon become clear. The more forceful
way was 6 P–Q4 etc.

6	B–KN5!
7 P–KR3	. . . .

White's desire to drive off the pinning Bishop is natural,
but . . .

7	P–KR4!?

99

An enticing offer which White should decline.

Position after 7 . . . P–KR4!?

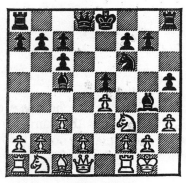

BLACK

WHITE

| 8 P×B? | .... |

White is not looking ahead.

| P×P | 8 .... |

Black's sacrifice has given him a mighty attacking line in the open King Rook file. And don't forget the looming possibility of . . . P–N6!

| 9 N×P | P–N6! |

Very menacing. If White tries 10 P–Q3, the result might be 10 . . . N×P!; 11 P×N, P×Pch; 12 R×P, Q×Q mate!

| 10 P–Q4 | .... |

Seemingly a conclusive answer, but Black is prepared for it.

| 10 .... | N×P! |

With this threat: 11 . . . R–R8ch!; 12 K×R, Q–R5ch; 13 K–N1, Q–R7 mate. White should try 11 P×P.

| 11 Q–N4? | B×P |

Another neat way to win is 11 . . . P×Pch; 12 R×P, R–R8ch!; 13 K×R, N×Rch and 14 . . . N×Q.

| 12 Q×N | B×Pch |

White resigns, not relishing the sequel 13 R×B, Q—Q8ch; 14 R—B1, R—R8ch!; 15 K×R, Q×R mate.

Black pounced on White's faulty 8th move to build up a winning attack with dizzying rapidity.

The Romantic Era of Chess

THE ROMANTIC MOVEMENT which was so influential in nineteenth-century art, literature and music also left its mark on chess. The games of this period are full of forceful attacks and slashing sacrifices. The following game is one of the masterpieces of the period.

RUY LOPEZ

Breslau, 1859

White	Black
ANDERSSEN	LANGE
1 P–K4	P–K4
2 N–KB3	N–QB3
3 B–N5	N–Q5
4 N×N	P×N
5 B–B4?	. . . .

Waste of time. Simply 5 Castles, N–B3; 6 P–K5 was in order.

5	N–B3
6 P–K5	P–Q4!

A formidable counter. On 7 P×N, P×B Black has a fine game.

| 7 B–N3 | . . . . |

Now the Bishop is buried alive, whereas the Black Knight goes on to great deeds.

| 7 . . . . | B–KN5! |

This involves the sacrifice of at least a piece.

8 P–KB3	N–K5!
9 Castles	. . . .

Or 9 P×B, Q–R5ch and White can choose between 10 K–K2?, Q–B7ch; 11 K–Q3, N–B4 mate or 10 P–N3, N×NP; 11 P×N, Q×Rch with a winning attack for Black.

Position after 9 Castles

BLACK

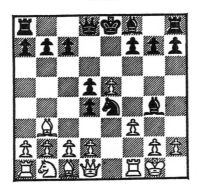

WHITE

9	P–Q6!

Black continues in the grand manner.

10 P×B	B–B4ch
11 K–R1	N–N6ch!
12 P×N	Q–N4

Black threatens . . . Q–R3 mate.

13 R–B5	P–KR4!

On 14 R×Q there follows 14 . . . P×P dis ch; 15 R–R5, R×R mate.

14 NP×P	Q×R

With the piquant threat 15 . . . Q–B8ch!; 16 Q×Q, R×P mate.

15 P–N4	R×Pch!
16 P×R	Q–K5

Threatens . . . Q–KR5 mate.

17	Q–B3	Q–KR5ch!
18	Q–R3	Q–K8ch
	Resigns	

Black has a forced mate: 19 K–R2, B–N8ch!; 20 K–R1, B–B7 dis ch; 21 K–R2, Q–N8 mate. A cascade of sacrifices. Note White's laggard development.

Modern Romanticism

THOUGH WE OFTEN hear complaints about the alleged dullness of twentieth-century chess, games like this one show that the old Romantic spirit still flourishes.

RUY LOPEZ

Vienna, 1934

White	*Black*
KMOCH	AMATEUR
1 P–K4	P–K4
2 N–KB3	N–QB3
3 B–N5	KN–K2
4 Castles	P–KN3

The logical sequel to Black's previous move, which has blocked the Bishop's natural development.

5 P–Q4	B–N2
6 P×P	N×P
7 N×N	B×N
8 B–KR6!?	. . . .

A very enterprising speculation. He offers a Pawn and the Exchange in order to get rid of Black's King Bishop.

8	B×NP
9 N–Q2	. . . .

In the event of 9 . . . B×R; 10 Q×B, KR–N1; 11 B–N5 White's mastery of the black squares will make Black's life miserable. Avoiding this, Black stumbles into something just as bad.

9	P–QB3
10 R–N1	B–Q5?
11 N–B4!	. . . .

White threatens 12 N—Q6 mate.

    11 . . . .   **B—B4**

All's well—he thinks.

Position after 11 . . . B—B4

BLACK

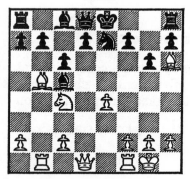

WHITE

    12 Q—Q4!!   **Resigns**

If 12 . . . B×Q; 13 N—Q6 mate. If 12 . . . KR—N1; 13 Q×B and White's Bishop is immune because of the renewed threat of N—Q6 mate. A sparkling miniature.

Child Prodigies

CHESS HAS HAD many child prodigies. The first of these, Paul Morphy, was undoubtedly the most glamorous and probably the ablest. In the following game, played when he was 13, he puts his grown-up opponent to shame.

FRENCH DEFENSE

New Orleans, 1850

White	Black
McCONNELL	MORPHY
1 P–K4	P–K3

This is the only known instance of Morphy's playing the French Defense. His genius was most happily displayed in the open games.

2 P–Q4	P–Q4
3 P–K5	P–QB4
4 P–QB3	N–QB3
5 P–KB4?	. . . .

A weak and weakening move. The alternative 5 N–B3 is preferable by far.

5	Q–N3
6 N–B3	B–Q2
7 P–QR3?	. . . .

Nor does this noticeably help matters along. He should have played 7 B–K2.

7	N–R3

In order to play . . . N–B4, increasing the pressure on White's Queen Pawn.

8 P–QN4	P×QP
9 P×P	R–B1!

Having developed with his customary rapidity, Morphy senses the possibilities along the Queen Bishop file.

10 B–N2	N–B4
11 Q–Q3	. . . .

This allows Black to bring off a neat combination, but it can hardly be considered a blunder since White is lost in any event.

Position after 11 Q–Q3

BLACK

WHITE

11	B×Pch!
12 P×B	N×NP
13 Q–Q2	. . . .

On 13 Q–Q1 Black has several ways to win, the simplest being 13 . . . N–B7ch and 14 . . . Q×B.

13	R–B7
14 Q–Q1	N–K6
Resigns	

White's Queen is trapped. Black has admirably exploited the resources of his superior position.

Time is of the Essence

EVERY NOW AND THEN some foolhardy player decides to capture a Pawn in exchange for lost time. When the experiment is fraught with danger—as it is here—we need not be surprised at the resulting quick, drastic finish.

FRENCH DEFENSE

London, 1954

White	*Black*
KERES	WADE
1 P–K4	P–K3
2 P–Q4	P–Q4
3 N–QB3	N–KB3
4 B–KN5	B–K2
5 P–K5	KN–Q2
6 P–KR4!	B×B
7 P×B	Q×P

In return for his Pawn White has a lead in development, a freer position, an open King Rook file, and the prospect of gaining time by attacking Black's Queen. Obviously White has a bargain.

8 N–R3	Q–K2
9 N–B4	P–QR3

Black wants to play . . . P–QB4 and therefore prevents the annoying reply N–N5 heading for Queen 6.

10 Q–N4	K–B1

Likewise after 10 . . . P–KN3; 11 Castles, P–QB4; 12 Q–N3! White has a dominant position (his threat is

13 KN×QP!, P×N; 14 N×P, Q–Q1; 15 P–K6! with an irresistible double threat).

11 **Q–B3!**	. . . .

Now White threatens to win at once with 12 N–N6ch.

11	**K–N1**
12 **B–Q3**	**P–QB4**

Here 12 . . . N–B1 is more solid.

Position after 12 . . . P–QB4

BLACK

WHITE

13 **B×Pch!**	**R×B**
14 **R×R**	**K×R**
15 **Castles**	. . . .

Black's best hope of putting up a fight at this stage lies in 15 . . . N–B1—for example 16 R–R1ch, K–N1; 17 R–R5, P–KB4; 18 Q–R3, K–B2; although after 19 P–KN4! Black will eventually cave in under the pressure.

15	**P–B4**

After this it's all over.

16 **R–R1ch**	**K–N1**
17 **R–R8ch!**	**Resigns**

For if 17 . . . K×R; 18 N–N6ch wins Black's Queen, white if 17 . . . K–B2; 18 Q–R5ch and mate next move. A good move example of the danger of wasting precious time. Note Black's undeveloped Queen-side pieces.

Static King, Gallivanting Queen

INSTEAD OF LEAVING his Queen at home and castling his King into safety, Black neglects castling and sends his Queen galloping around the board. The consequences are grievous.

FRENCH DEFENSE

Riga, 1913

White	Black
NINZOVICH	ALAPIN
1 P–K4	P–K3
2 P–Q4	P–Q4
3 N–QB3	N–KB3
4 P×P	N×P
5 N–B3	P–QB4
6 N×N	Q×N

The Black Queen starts on her travels.

7 B–K3!	P×P
8 N×P	P–QR3
9 B–K2	Q×NP?

He falls in with White's plans.

10 B–B3	Q–N3
11 Q–Q2	P–K4

Position after 11 . . . P–K4

BLACK

WHITE

| 12 Castles(Q)!! | . . . . |

White correctly estimates that his enormous lead in development is worth a piece.

| 12 . . . . | P×N |
| 13 B×QP | . . . . |

White threatens 14 B×KNP!, B×B; 15 Q–Q8 mate.

| 13 . . . . | N–B3 |
| 14 B–B6!! | . . . . |

Sheer genius. His threat is 15 Q–Q8ch!, N×Q; 16 R×N mate.

| 14 . . . . | Q×B |

Against such moves as 14 . . . P×B or . . . B–K3 White mates quickly beginning with 15 B×Nch. Even 14 . . . B–K2 is useless: 15 B×Nch, P×B; 16 Q–Q8ch!, B×Q; 17 R×B mate.

| 15 KR–K1ch | B–K2 |

Or 15 . . . B–K3; 16 Q–Q7 mate.

| 16 B×Nch | K–B1 |

He sees that 16 . . . Q×B allows 17 Q–Q8 mate.

| 17 Q–Q8ch! | B×Q |
| 18 R–K8 mate | |

White took admirable advantage of Black's mishandling of his King and Queen.

Blindfold Play

FEW FACETS of master chess are more attractive than the great player's flair for playing without sight of board and men. Here is one of the finest games ever produced in this field.

FRENCH DEFENSE

Tarnopol, 1916)

(White plays blindfold)

White ALEKHINE	Black FELDT
1 P–K4	P–K3
2 P–Q4	P–Q4
3 N–QB3	N–KB3
4 P×P	N×P

The reply 4 . . . P×P is better because it maintains control of the center.

5 N–K4	P–KB4?

Bad. Black creates a "hole" at his King 4 square—it is no longer commanded by his Pawns. In addition, his King Pawn becomes backward—it can no longer be defended by his Pawns.

6 N–N5!	B–K2
7 N/N5–B3	P–B3
8 N–K5	. . . .

White occupies the hole.

8	. . . .	Castles
9	N/N1–B3	P–QN3
10	B–Q3	B–N2
11	Castles	R–K1
12	P–B4	N–B3
13	B–B4	QN–Q2
14	Q–K2	P–B4

A better defense—at least for the time being—was 14 . . . N–B1 or 14 . . . B–KB1. But who could expect Black to foresee what was coming?

Position after 14 . . . P–B4

BLACK

WHITE

15 N–B7!!   . . . .

This move is as powerful as it is unexpected. Black must capture, as his Queen and feeble King Pawn are menaced.

15 . . . .   K×N
16 Q×Pch!!   . . . .

The real point—if 16 . . . K×Q; 17 N–N5 mate. And if 16 . . . K–B1; 17 N–N5 crushes Black.

16 . . . .   K–N3

Alekhine announced mate in two:

17 P–KN4!   B–K5

To stop 18 B × P mate.

18 **N–R4 mate**

What is so profoundly satisfying about White's exquisite 16 Q × Pch!! is that it is the direct exploitation of Black's feeble 5 . . . P–KB4?

Deceptive Aggression

ONE OF THE MOST INTERESTING facets of a great master's art is his knack of demolishing positions which seem overwhelming. It required the keenest kind of insight on Black's part to convince himself that White's imposing-looking position was really hollow.

FRENCH DEFENSE

London, 1923

White	Black
WHITEHEAD	MAROCZY
1 P–K4	P–K3
2 P–Q4	P–Q4
3 N–QB3	N–KB3
4 P–K5	KN–Q2

Black will try to undermine White powerful-looking Pawn center with . . . P–QB4 and . . . P–KB3. White will support his Pawn center with P–QB3 and P–KB4. This explains his next move, which is a preparation for P–QB3.

5 QN–K2	P–QB4
6 P–QB3	N–QB3
7 P–KB4	Q–N3
8 N–B3	P–B3!
9 P–KN3	. . . .

White hopes to play B–N2 but never quite gets to it. White's support of his center gets his pieces entangled; Black's attack on the center opens up lines for him.

9	QBP×P
10 BP×P	P×P
11 BP×P	B–N5ch

The best reply to this is 12 N—B3. White's reply leads to quick trouble.

12 K—B2?   **Castles**

Interestingly enough this matter-of-fact move threatens . . . N×KP as both White's Queen Pawn and King Knight are pinned.

13 B—K3   • • • •

Position after 13 B—K3

BLACK

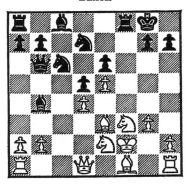

WHITE

13 . . . .   **N/Q2×P!!**

The unexpected start of a dynamic breakthrough.

14 P×N   **R×Nch!!**
15 K×R   **N×Pch**

Leaving White very little choice, for on 16 K—B2 the reply 16 . . . N—N5ch is deadly. For example: 17 K—B3, Q×Bch!; 18 K×N, P—K4 dis ch with mate next move.

16 K—B4   **Q—Q3!**

Conclusive, but an attractive alternative line was 16 . . . P—N4ch! and if 17 K×N, B—Q3ch; 18 K—B6, Q—Q1 mate!

17 B—R3   • • • •

A pretty alternative is 17 B—Q4, Q—B1ch; 18 K—K3, Q—B6 mate.

17 . . . .   **B—Q2**

And here 17 . . . Q–B1ch also does the trick.

18 B–Q4   R–B1ch

White resigns, just in time to avoid 19 K–N5, Q–K2ch; 20 K–R5, B–K1 mate.

As pointed out in the note to White's ninth move, Black's assault on the Pawn center went hand in hand with the forceful development of his pieces.

Sacrificing on Spec

ONE OF THE MOST pleasing forms of attacking play is seen in speculative sacrifices which are made intuitively. To be able to sense the potentialities in a position is one of the hallmarks of a master.

FRENCH DEFENSE

Lodz, 1929

White	Black
NAIDORF	SAPIRO
1 P–K4	P–K3
2 P–Q4	P–Q4
3 N–QB3	P×P

A listless continuation that always gives White a much freer game.

4 N×P	N–Q2
5 N–KB3	KN–B3
6 B–Q3	B–K2
7 Castles	P–QN3

An ill timed move. Castling is much safer at this point.

8 N–K5!	. . . .

White threatens nothing less than winning the Black Queen with N–B6.

8	B–N2
9 N×Nch	P×N?

This exposes the Black King to a withering attack. The alternative 9 . . . B×N was safer though not inviting.

10 N×P‼	. . . .

Here is an intuitive sacrifice based on the insecure position of Black's King.

| 10 . . . . | K×N |
| 11 **Q–R5ch** | K–N1 |

Other King moves would be senseless as White would reply 12 B–R6ch getting a new piece into the attack without loss of time.

| 12 **R–K1** | N–B1 |

The alternative 12 . . . B–Q4 is futile because of 13 P–QB4 driving off the Bishop.

Position after 12 . . . N–B1

BLACK

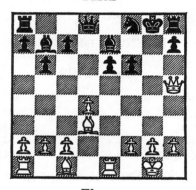

WHITE

13 R×P‼ . . . .

A second surprising sacrifice, and apparently quite sound. White's enterprise is all the more commendable since he could have won in more conservative fashion with 13 B–KR6, P–KB4 (to prevent Q–N4ch); 14 R–K3!, Q–K1; 15 R–N3ch, N–N3; 16 B–QB4 etc.

13	N×R
14 **B–QB4**	Q–Q3
15 **B–KR6**	. . . .

White threatens to win by 16 Q–N4ch, K–B2; 17 Q–N7ch! etc.

| 15 . . . . | B–KB1 |
| 16 **R–K1** | . . . . |

With this neat possibility: 16 . . . B×B; 17 B×Nch,
K–N2; 18 Q–B7 mate.

16	**B–B1**
17 Q–K8!	. . . .

Now White threatens to win with 18 R×N!

17	**B–Q2**

Desperation.

18 **R×N!!**	**R×Q**
19 **R×R dis ch**	**B–K3**
20 **B×Bch**	**Q×B**
21 **R×B mate**	

Once given his opportunity for a speculative sacrifice,
White never relaxed the pressure. His appraisal of the
prospects of success was uncannily accurate.

A Modern Miracle

THE CHARMED LIFE of White's stranded Knight at Queen
Rook 8 verges on the miraculous. It becomes less of a
miracle when we see the marvelous ingenuity that White
lavishes on the problem.

SICILIAN DEFENSE

Amsterdam, 1954

White	*Black*
KERES	SAITAR
1 P–K4	P–QB4
2 N–KB3	P–Q3
3 P–Q4	P×P
4 N×P	N–KB3
5 N–QB3	P–QR3
6 B–KN5	QN–Q2
7 B–QB4	P–K3

More energetic is 7 . . . N–N3; 8 B–N3, P–K4; 9
N–B3, B–K3.

8 Castles	Q–B2

Even now it was not too late for . . . N–N3 etc. But
Black seems blissfully unaware of the explosive potentialities of the position.

Position after 8 . . . Q–B2

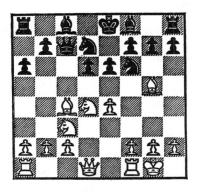

9 B×KP!	P×B
10 N×P	Q–B5
11 N–Q5!	. . . .

A hidden point is that after 11 . . . N×N; 12 P×N, N–K4 Black's Queen can be driven off: 13 P–QN3, Q–B6; 14 B–Q2, Q–N7; 15 N–B7ch winning the Queen Rook.

11	K–B2
12 B×N	. . . .

A difficult move to answer, for if 12 . . . P×B; 13 Q–R5ch! with a mating attack. Or 12 . . . N×B; 13 P–QN3, Q–N4; 14 N/K6–B7 and wins.

12	K×N
13 B–B3!	. . . .

And now the powerful threat of Q–B3–B5 mate wins more material.

13	N–B3
14 B×N	P×B
15 N–N6	Q–B3
16 N×R	. . . .

This Knight has a charmed life. If 16 . . . P–N3; 17 N×P!, Q×N; 18 Q–N4ch, followed by 19 Q×B.

16	B–K2

Now that Black's Queen Bishop is protected by his Rook, the threat of . . . P—N3 is real.

    17 P—QR4!   **. . . .**

Threatening P—R5, assuring the Knight's escape.

17	**P—N3**
18 Q—Q5ch!	**K—Q2**
19 R—R3!	**. . . .**

And now if 19 . . . B—N2; 20 R—QB3!, Q×Q; 21 N×Pch wins for White.

19	**B—Q1**
20 N×Pch!	**Resigns**

White has the last laugh. If 20 . . . Q×N; 21 Q—KB5ch, K—B2; 22 R—QB3ch wins; or if 20 . . . B×N; 21 Q—B7ch, K—Q1; 22 Q×BPch winning the Rook. An enchanting finale.

Too Many Queen Moves

OCCASIONALLY A PLAYER is so fascinated with the power of the Queen that he makes altogether too many moves with this valuable piece. In the present game this results in a debacle shortly after the opening phase.

SICILIAN DEFENSE

USSR Championship Semi-Finals, 1954

White	*Black*
CHERBAKOV	TAIMANOV
1 P–K4	P–QB4
2 N–KB3	N–QB3
3 P–Q4	P×P
4 N×P	N–B3
5 N–QB3	P–Q3
6 B–KN5	P–K3
7 Q–Q3	• • • •

White wants to castle Queen-side early.

7 • • • •	P–QR3
8 Castles	B–Q2
9 P–B4	P–R3
10 B–R4	• • • •

Position after 10 B—R4

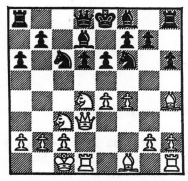

BLACK

WHITE

10 ....   P—KN4!

Well played. By liquidating White's King Bishop Pawn, Black gains permanent control of his King 4 square.

| 11 P×P | N—KN5! |
| 12 Q—N3 | P×P |

The idea is that on 13 Q×N Black can reply 13 . . . R×B with a distinct positional plus because of his two Bishops and his command of the King 4 square. In his anxiety to avoid this, White falls into something much worse.

13 N—B3??	P×B
14 Q×N	P—K4!
Resigns	

It is finis for the White Queen. The only available move is 15 Q—N5, but then 15 . . . B—R3 wins the Queen.

Playful Strangulation

THANKS TO BLACK's inept opening play White ties him up in knots with a series of playful Knight moves. Moral: never develop pieces backwards.

SICILIAN DEFENSE

Budapest, 1942

White	Black
KLUGER	NAGY
1 P–K4	P–QB4
2 N–KB3	N–QB3
3 P–Q4	P×P
4 N×P	N–B3
5 N–QB3	P–Q3
6 B–KN5	P–QR3

Here 6 . . . P–K3 is perfectly acceptable.

7 Q–Q2	N–Q2?

This retreat is incomprehensible as 7 . . . P–K3 still leaves Black with a playable game.

8 B–K2	P–KN3
9 N–Q5!	. . . .

Position after 9 N–Q5!

BLACK

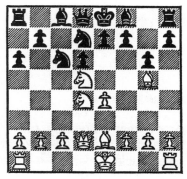

WHITE

White has set an amusing trap: if Black plays the plausible 9 . . . B–N2? there follows 10 N×N, P×N; 11 B×KP and Black's Queen is lost.

Likewise after 9 . . . P–R3; 10 B–R4, P–KN4 we get 11 N–K6!, P×N; 12 B–R5 mate—or 11 . . . Q–R4; 12 Q×Q, N×Q; 13 N/Q5–B7 mate!

9	P–B3
10 N–K6	Q–R4

What follows is delightful—though not for Black.

11 N/Q5–B7ch	K–B2
12 N–Q8ch	K–N2
13 N–K8ch	Resigns

Black can do without 13 . . . K–N1; 14 B–QB4ch followed by mate. An extraordinary finish.

Reluctant Dragon

THE DRAGON VARIATION of the Sicilian Defense calls for energetic and precise play on Black's part. Lacking such a policy, he can easily fall by the wayside.

SICILIAN DEFENSE

Match, 1893

White	*Black*
DR. LASKER	GOLMAYO
1 P–K4	P–QB4
2 N–KB3	P–KN3
3 P–Q4	P×P
4 N×P	B–N2
5 N–QB3	N–QB3
6 B–K3	N–B3
7 B–K2	Castles
8 P–B4	P–Q3
9 Castles	. . . .

Here 9 N–N3 (more accurate) would transpose into the Alekhine-Botvinnik game on page 132.

9	N–KN5?

Instead, 9 . . . Q–N3!?, with various tactical threats, is the move.

10 B×N	. . . .

A trap: if Black replies 10 . . . B×B? White wins a piece with 11 N×N!

10	B×N
11 B/K3×B	B×B
12 Q–Q2!	B–K3

The Bishop retreats before White shuts off its retreat with 13 P–B5.

13 **P–B5**	**B–B5**
14 **R–B3!**	....

White threatens a mating attack with R–R3 and Q–R6. Black therefore deflects the White Queen by means of:

14	**N×B**
15 **Q×N**	....

Thanks to the previous exchange, White's Queen has taken up a commanding position. However, if Black forces the exchange of Queens with 15 . . . Q–N3 he comes out a Pawn down (16 Q×Q, P×Q; 17 P–QN3, B–R3; 18 N–Q5!).

15	**B–R3**
16 **N–Q5!**	....

Position after 16 N–Q5!

BLACK

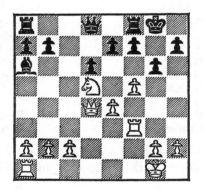

WHITE

The powerful centralization of the Knight gives White overwhelming command of the board. For example, on 16 . . . P–B3 he has a winning reply in 17 N–B4! Or consider 16 . . . P–K3; 17 P×KP, P×P; 18 N–B6ch and Black must give up the Exchange with 18 . . . R×N.

16	**R–B1**
17 **P–B6!**	....

With this possibility: 17 . . . P–K3; 18 N–K7ch,
K–R1; 19 Q–K3! (playing for mate), R–KN1; 20
R–R3 (threatens R×Pch!), Q–B1; 21 N×QR!, Q×N;
22 R×Pch!, K×R; 23 Q–KR3 mate.

17	R–B5
18 Q–Q2!	P×P
19 Q–R6	P–B4
20 R–KR3	Resigns

Black is helpless against the coming mate. His care-
lessness in the opening left him without counterplay.

"Only A Draw"

THOUGH MANY DRAWN GAMES are unbearably dull, this one is the proverbial exception. Both players are out for blood, and the drawn result is the logical outcome of mutual exhaustion.

SICILIAN DEFENSE

Nottingham, 1936

White	*Black*
ALEKHINE	BOTVINNIK
1 P–K4	P–QB4
2 N–KB3	P–Q3
3 P–Q4	P×P
4 N×P	N–KB3
5 N–QB3	P–KN3

The popular Dragon Variation.

6 B–K2	B–N2
7 B–K3	N–B3
8 N–N3	B–K3
9 P–B4	Castles

So far the game has proceeded in conventional vein, and now one would expect the equally routine 10 Castles.

10 P–N4!?	. . . .

This violent thrust completely changes the character of the game. If Black plays passively, White will continue P–N5 followed by P–KR4–5 with a terrific attack.

10	P–Q4!

132

An energetic counter which tells us that Black means to fight back.

11	P–B5!		B–B1!
12	KP×P		N–N5

Now it seems that Black will win back his Pawn with a good game, unless White goes in for 13 P×P, RP×P; 14 B–B3. In that case Black proceeds vigorously with 14 . . . N×NP!; 15 B×N, B×B; 16 Q×B, N×Pch with a free-for-all.

Position after 12 . . . N–N5

BLACK

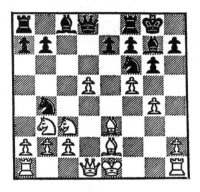

WHITE

13 P–Q6!   . . . .

Another surprise—and a powerful-looking move to boot. Main point: if 13 . . . KP×P?; 14 P–N5, N–K1; 15 P–B6 and Black's King Bishop is nailed in for good.

13 . . . .   Q×P!

Black is commendably alert. His idea is that on 14 Q×Q, P×Q; 15 P–N5 he has 15 . . . KN–Q4! gaining time by his counterattack on White's loose Bishop to stave off P–B6.

14 B–B5!   . . . .

Now it seems that Black has nothing better than 14 . . . Q×Qch; 15 R×Q, N–B3; 16 P–N5, N–Q2; 17 P–B6, B–R1 (after 17 . . . N×B; 18 P×B! Black

133

loses material); 18 B–R3, R–K1; but then 19 N–Q5 gives White a clearly winning game.

14	Q–B5!!

Magnificent play. Black willingly parts with a piece or two in order to salvage the game.

15 R–KB1	Q×RP
16 B×N	N×P!!

If White turns up his nose at this Knight by playing 17 B–B5, there follows 17 . . . Q–N6ch; 18 B–B2, N×B; 19 R×N, B×P and Black has very strong pressure.

17 B×N	Q–N6ch

White must take the draw, for 18 K–K2? is answered by 18 . . . Q×Bch, while 18 K–Q2? will not do because of 18 . . . B–R3ch. In either case Black would win.

18 R–B2	Q–N8ch

The game was abandoned as a draw, neither player being in a position to vary. Only Black's determined and energetic resistance saved him from defeat.

A Bad Plan is Better?

A BAD PLAN is better than none at all, they say. But games like this one prove how fatuous this platitude is.

SICILIAN DEFENSE

Postal Game, 1922

White	*Black*
L. STEINER	SZABAY
1 P–K4	P–QB4
2 N–KB3	N–KB3

With the same provocative idea as in Alekhine's Defense. But White refuses to advance his King Pawn.

3 N–B3	P–Q4
4 P×P	N×P
5 N–K5	N×N
6 NP×N	Q–Q4
7 B–N5ch	N–Q2

White can save his threatened Pawn by 8 N×N, B×N; 9 B×Bch, Q×B. But this far-reaching simplification is neither attractive nor powerful, so he prefers something more adventurous.

8 Q–K2!	Q×NP?

This meets with an astounding refutation. He had a much safer alternative in 8 . . . P–QR3, forcing some liquidation.

BLACK

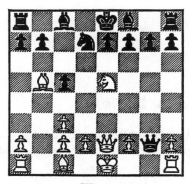

WHITE

9 Q–Q3!	. . . .

White doesn't bother to defend his threatened Rook.

9	Q×Rch
10 K–K2	P–K3
11 B×Nch	K–K2

Forced.

12 B×B	R×B
13 Q–Q7ch	K–B3

Black hopes for 14 Q×R, Q–K5ch—which gives him a perpetual check. But of course nothing could be further from White's mind.

14 Q×BPch!	K×N
15 P–Q4ch	. . . .

A charming situation. On 15 . . . P×P or 15 . . . K–Q3 White wins the Black Queen with 16 B–B4ch, while 15 . . . K–K5 allows 16 Q×KP mate.

15	K–Q4
16 Q×NPch	R–B3

Black does not fancy 16 . . . K–B5; 17 Q–N3 mate.

17 P–QB4ch	Resigns

For after 17 . . . K×BP; 18 Q–N3ch, K×P White wins the Black Queen with 19 B–N2ch or 19 B–K3ch. Black's determined execution of a bad plan led directly to a lost game.

Danish Gambit Revisited

WHITE PERFORMS a conjurer's trick: he turns a Sicilian Defense into a Danish Gambit. With Black's help, the speculation turns out famously.

SICILIAN DEFENSE

Warsaw, 1935

	White	*Black*
	KERES	WINTER
1	P–K4	P–QB4
2	N–KB3	N–KB3
3	P–K5	N–Q4
4	N–B3	P–K3

Here 4 . . . N×N is simpler and safer.

5	N×N	P×N
6	P–Q4	P–Q3
7	B–N5!	Q–R4ch

The obvious 7 . . . B–K2 loses a Pawn after 8 B×B, Q×B; 9 P×BP etc.

8	P–B3	BP×P
9	B–Q3!?	. . . .

Throwing Pawns to the wind, White plays for a dashing Danish-type attack.

9	. . . .	P×BP
10	Castles	P×NP?

But this is too much of a good thing. The alternative 10 . . . N–B3; 11 R–K1, B–K3 was much safer.

| 11 | R–N1 | P×P? |

This only enhances White's attacking prospects. Instead, 11 . . . B–K3 should have been tried.

12 N×P   B–Q3

Of course, on 12 . . . P–B3; 13 Q–R5ch is devastating.

Position after 12 . . . B–Q3

BLACK

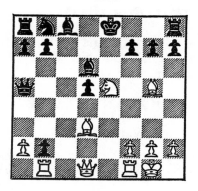

WHITE

13 N×P‼   K×N
14 Q–R5ch   . . . .

Black's King is in a very shaky state, for example 14 . . . K–K3; 15 B–B5ch!, K–K4; 16 KR–K1ch, K–Q5; 17 B–K3ch, K–B6; 18 Q–Q1! and Black can resign.

14 . . . .   P–KN3

Conservative retreat is no better: 14 . . . K–B1; 15 KR–K1 (threatens mate), B–Q2; 16 Q–B3ch, K–N1; 17 B–K7 and White wins.

15 B×Pch!   P×B
16 Q×R   B–KB4

Nor is 16 . . . N–Q2 satisfactory: 17 Q–R7ch, K–B1; 18 B–R6ch, K–K1; 19 Q×Pch etc.

17 QR–K1   B–K5

An interesting alternative is 17 . . . B–KB1; 18 R–

138

K7ch!, B×R; 19 Q–R7ch, K–B1; 20 Q×Bch, K–N1;
21 B–B6 with a mating position.

| 18 R×B!! | P×R |
| 19 Q–B6ch | Resigns |

If Black tries 19 . . . K–K1 he is mated in two
moves. On 19 . . . K–N1 there follows 20 Q×Pch,
K–B1; 21 Q×Bch, K–N1; 22 Q–K6ch!, K–N2; 23
Q–K7ch! with a quick mate in the offing. The con-
centrated fury of White's onslaught was amazing.

Why Interpolate?

THE FATE OF many a game is changed when a previously calculated line of play is given a completely different turn through the interpolation of some unforeseen move. A happy inspiration of this kind will often save a game that would otherwise have been lost. Failure to find one of these moves will often lose a game that could have been saved.

SICILIAN DEFENSE

Hamburg, 1954

White	*Black*
RELLSTAB	SEEGEBRECHT
1 P–K4	P–QB4
2 N–KB3	P–Q3
3 P–B3	N–KB3
4 B–Q3	. . . .

A peculiar-looking move, as the Bishop now blocks White's Queen Pawn. The idea is to protect his King Pawn while he prepares to set up a broad Pawn center with P–Q4 (after B–B2). Black has ample resources, however.

4	N–B3
5 B–B2	B–N5
6 P–KR3	B–R4
7 P–Q4	P–K3
8 P–Q5	N–K4

This is playable, but 8 . . . P×P; 9 P×P, N–K4 is a much safer sequence.

9 B–R4ch	N/B3–Q2

After 9 . . . N/K4–Q2; 10 P×P, P×P; 11 Q–N3 White's double attack wins a Pawn.

    10 P×P   . . . .

Position after 10 P×P

BLACK

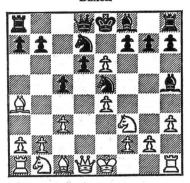

WHITE

    10 . . . .   P×P?

This allows White to win in brilliant fashion. It was vital for Black to interpolate the important move 10 . . . N×Nch! with this possible continuation: 11 P×N, P×P; 12 Q–N3, B×P; 13 Q×KPch, Q–K2; 14 B×Nch, K–Q1; 15 R–N1, Q×B.

    11 N×N!   . . . .

The first point that Black missed.

    11 . . . .   B×Q
    12 B×Nch   . . . .

And here is the second point that Black missed: 12 . . . K–K2 is answered by 13 B–KN5 mate.

    12 . . . .   Q×B
    13 N×Q   B–B7
    14 N×B   Resigns

Black has lost a piece. The play at move 10 is highly instructive.

Vital Statistics

THE STATISTICALLY MINDED READER will be interested to know that six of Black's 14 moves in this game were Pawn moves; the remaining eight were King moves. It is easy to guess the outcome.

SICILIAN DEFENSE

Helsinki, 1944

White	Black
KROGIUS	OJANEN
1 P–K4	P–QB4
2 P–Q4	P×P
3 N–KB3	....

There is no better way of confusing one's opponent than by turning a humdrum opening into a gambit. Black is well advised to return to the familiar paths with 3 . . . N–QB3 or 3 . . . P–Q3.

| 3 .... | P–K4 |

Now we have a real gambit, as White dare not play 4 N×KP? because of 4 . . . Q–R4ch winning the Knight.

| 4 P–B3! | P×P |
| 5 N×BP | .... |

It is already clear that Black will be condemned to passivity, partly because of his backward development, partly because of his unfavorably placed Queen Pawn.

| 5 .... | P–Q3 |
| 6 B–QB4 | P–KR3 |

This makes a very bad impression, but Black is afraid to play 6 . . . N–KB3 because of the annoying reply 7 N–KN5. However, his King Bishop Pawn is more vulnerable than he realizes.

Position after 6 . . . P–KR3

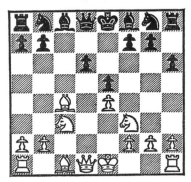

| 7 B×Pch! | K×B |
| 8 N×Pch | . . . . |

The fact that Black's Queen Pawn is pinned is what makes this attack possible.

Black has no really satisfactory reply, as 8 . . . K–K1 allows 9 Q–R5ch with mate to follow.

On 8 . . . K–K3 White continues 9 Q–Q5ch, K–B3; 10 Q–B7ch, K×N; 11 B–B4ch and mate next move.

In the event of 8 . . . K–B3 White plays 9 Q–Q4! (threatens 10 N–B6 dis ch), Q–K1; 10 N–Q5ch, K–K3; 11 N–QB7ch winning Black's Queen.

8	K–K2
9 N–Q5ch	K–K3
10 Q–N4ch!	. . . .

The hunt is on in earnest.

| 10 . . . . | K×N |
| 11 B–B4ch | K–Q5 |

Or 11 . . . K×P; 12 N–B3ch, K–Q5; 13 Q–Q1ch, K–B5; 14 Q–N3ch, K–Q5; 15 Q–Q5 mate.

| 12 B–K3ch! | K–K4 |

On 12 . . . K–B5; 13 Q–K2 mate makes a pretty tableau.

13 Q–B4ch   K–K3
14 Q–B5 mate

White energetically exploited Black's shortcomings.

Modern Gambits

IN MODERN TIMES all sorts of staid openings have been turned into gambits. The idea is to confront the opponent with surprises so unpleasant that he is at a loss for the proper reply.

SICILIAN DEFENSE

Helsinki, 1936

White	Black
KERES	GAUFFIN
1 P–K4	P–QB4
2 N–KB3	P–QR3
3 P–QN4!?	. . . .

There we have it. White seeks rapid development.

3	P×P
4 P–QR3	P–Q4
5 KP×P	Q×P
6 P×P	B–N5

Black would be better off to develop his King-side forces and castle into safety.

7 N–B3	Q–KR4

And here the retreat 7 . . . Q–Q1 is more prudent.

8 B–K2	P–K3
9 Castles	N–KB3
10 R–R5!!	. . . .

Unorthodox but powerful. The reply 10 . . . P–QN4 will not do because of 11 B×Pch. Or if 10 . . . Q–N3;

11 R—KN5, Q—R3; 12 P—Q4 with the terrible threat of
13 R×B.

10	N—Q4
11 P—R3!	B×N

After this practically forced exchange, White's King
Bishop becomes very powerful.

12 B×B	N×N
13 P×N	Q—N3
14 Q—Q4!	. . . .

White threatens to win a whole Rook with 15 B×P.

14	Q—B3
15 Q—QB4	N—Q2

White was threatening dire destruction with Q—B8ch.

16 B—N5	. . . .

Position after 16 B—N5

Black seems to have an excellent resource in 16 . . .
N—K4—but in that case White replies 17 R×N!, Q×R;
18 Q—B6ch!!, P×Q; 19 B×P mate!

16	Q—N3
17 B×P	QR—N1
18 B—QB6	B—K2
19 B×Nch	K×B
20 R—Q1ch	Resigns

146

On 20 . . . K–K1; 21 Q–B7 is murderous. And on 20 . . . B–Q3 there follows 21 R×Bch!, K×R; 22 Q–B5ch, K–Q2; 23 Q–K7ch with mate to follow. Black never had a chance to catch his breath.

Lost Initiative

THOUGH WHITE is supposed to have a theoretical advantage in the first move, it does not take much to reverse roles. This is particularly true when the Black pieces are handled by a great master.

SICILIAN DEFENSE

St. Petersburg, 1912

White	*Black*
POTEMKIN	ALEKHINE
1 P–K4	P–QB4
2 P–KN3	P–KN3
3 B–N2	B–N2
4 N–K2	N–QB3
5 P–QB3	. . . .

White's hope of establishing a broad Pawn center with this move and P–Q4 turns out to be too ambitious, and his next move (intending N–B2) is too slow.

5	N–B3
6 N–R3	P–Q4!
7 P×P	N×P
8 N–B2	Castles
9 P–Q4	P×P
10 P×P	B–N5

Having snatched the initiative, Black never lets up the pressure from now on.

11 P–B3	B–B4

Threatens to win a Pawn with . . . B×N etc.

12 N–K3	Q–R4ch!

A neat point, for on 13 Q–Q2 or 13 B–Q2 Black wins
a piece with 13 . . . N×N!

13 K–B2	N/Q4–N5
14 N×B	Q×N
15 P–N4	N–Q6ch!
16 K–N3	. . . .

Position after 16 K–N3

BLACK

WHITE

16 . . . .   N×QP!

This is really a glamorous way to win a Pawn, as
White should go in for 17 N×N, Q–K4ch when Black
would regain the piece and win without much trouble.
Instead, White prefers to throw himself on his sword.

17 P×Q   N×BPch

Black announced mate in two: 18 K–N4, P–KR4ch
etc. Or 18 K–R3, N–B7 mate—a "picture mate." Black
never permitted his opponent a moment's rest.

The Hobgoblin

EMERSON ONCE REMARKED that a foolish consistency is the hobgoblin of little minds. Black's rigorous consistency leads to his resignation on the ninth move.

CARO-KANN DEFENSE

Duesseldorf, 1937

White	Black
ENGELS	MAY
1 P–K4	P–QB3
2 P–Q4	P–Q4
3 P×P	P×P
4 P–QB4	B–B4

This is out of place because after Black's next move he will lose valuable time. It is also questionable whether the Bishop should leave the Queen-side at this early stage.

5 P×P	Q×P
6 N–QB3	Q–QR4
7 Q–N3	. . . .

Position after 7 Q–N3

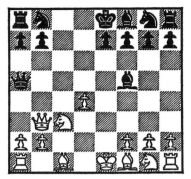

Black's comparatively best course is to play 7 . . . B–B1. But, rather than admit that he was wrong, he plays a move that leaves him with a hopeless game.

7	Q–N3?
8 N–Q5!	Q×Q
9 P×Q	Resigns

Black has no adequate reply to the double threat of 10 N–B7ch and 10 N–N6.

Stuck

RARELY DO WE SEE so tragicomical a position as the one
in which White resigns. Both Knights are pinned, and
White can never free himself.

CARO-KANN DEFENSE

Oslo, 1952

White	*Black*
ESPELI	ANDERSEN
1 P–K4	P–QB3
2 P–QB4	P–Q4
3 BP×P	P×P
4 B–N5ch	. . . .

Waste of time; 4 P×P is much better.

4	B–Q2
5 Q–R4?	. . . .

It is no exaggeration to say that this is the losing move.
White never recovers from his losses of time.

5	P×P
6 B×Bch	N×B!
7 Q×KP	N–B4
8 Q–QB4	N–Q6ch
9 K–K2	R–B1!

Every move a menace.

10 Q×N	Q×Qch
11 K×Q	R×B
12 K–K2	P–KN3!
Resigns	

BLACK

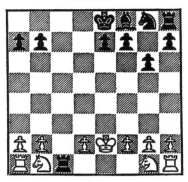

WHITE

White is unable to move either Rook or either Knight, and it is unclear when he will be able to do so.

Black's immediate threat is . . . B—N2 winning a Rook. The most likely line of play is therefore 13 P—Q4, B—N2; 14 K—Q2, B—R3ch; 15 K—K2, N—B3; 16 P—KN3, Castles; 17 K—B3, KR—B1; 18 K—N2, R/B1—B7 and Black has a very easy win. Black took drastic advantage of the opportunities offered him.

Low Bridge!

DESPITE THE POPULAR MISCONCEPTIONS about chess as a slow, tedious game it is possible to lose a full-blown tournament encounter in an alarmingly short time.

CARO-KANN DEFENSE

Plymouth, 1938

White	Black
ALEKHINE	BRUCE
1 P–K4	P–QB3
2 N–QB3	P–Q4
3 N–B3	. . . .

It is more usual to play 2 P–Q4 or 3 P–Q4, but the development of the two Knights has tricky features.

3	P×P
4 N×P	B–B4?

A serious mistake. The alternative 4 . . . B–N5 is preferable.

5 N–N3	B–N3?

And this plausible retreat makes matters worse. It was still possible to play . . . B–N5 despite the loss of time involved.

6 P–KR4!	P–KR3

Black creates a retreat for his Bishop.

7 N–K5!	. . . .

White threatens to compromise Black's Pawn position with 8 N×B etc.

7	B–R2
8 Q–R5	. . . .

And now White threatens mate on the move.

8 . . . .   P–KN3

Black buries his unfortunate Bishop alive—not that he has any choice.

Position after 8 . . . P–KN3

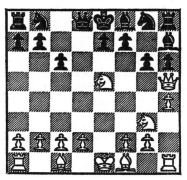

WHITE

9 B–B4!   . . . .

With this neat point: if Black plays 9 . . . P×Q White replies 10 B×P mate.

9 . . . .   P–K3
10 Q–K2   . . . .

With a new threat that Black misses—though his game is hopeless anyway.

10 . . . .   N–B3
11 N×KBP!   K×N
12 Q×Pch   Resigns

For after 12 . . . K–N2 there follows 13 Q–B7 mate.

First Things First

NOTHING IS SO DANGEROUS in the opening as trying to carry out far-reaching plans before completing one's development. This is just what Black tries to do here, and it is no surprise that he comes a cropper.

ALEKHINE'S DEFENSE

Des Moines, 1950

White	Black
ADAMS	AMATEUR
1 P–K4	N–KB3
2 P–K5	N–Q4
3 P–Q4	P–Q3
4 P–QB4	N–N3
5 P–B4	. . . .

In advancing his Pawns so readily White has taken a calculated risk. True, his center Pawns may become weak; but White reasons that this is a chance worth taking in order to drive Black's Knight to a very inferior post.

5	P×P
6 BP×P	P–KN3
7 B–K3	B–N2

Black's plan is clear. He has played the Bishop to King Knight 2 in order to undermine White's King Pawn with . . . P–QB4. This is an excellent strategical plan but it does not take account of possible tactical complications.

8 N–QB3	P–QB4

See the previous note. On the surface this is a good move, but it would have been much sounder to castle at

156

this point, safeguarding the Black King against any unpleasant eventualities.

Position after 8 . . . P—QB4

BLACK

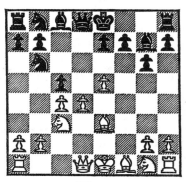

WHITE

| 9 P—Q5 | . . . . |

Comparatively best for Black now is 9 . . . B×P; 10 B×P etc., although the prospects for his Knights would have been rather poor.

| 9 . . . . | Q—B2? |

Black is too ambitious: he wants to win White's King Pawn without parting with his own Queen Bishop Pawn, and this is asking for too much.

| 10 P—Q6! | . . . . |

White immediately seizes on the opportunity to create favorable complications.

10	P×P
11 N—N5!	Q—K2
12 N×QPch	K—B1
13 N×B!	N×N
14 B×P!!	Resigns

For if Black captures the Bishop, White replies 15 Q—Q8 mate. Black has been made to pay a heavy price for his faulty plunge into tactical complications before safeguarding his King.

White Is Black and Right Is Wrong

TO THE PASSIONATE DEVOTEE OF CHESS nothing is more distressing than to see a player achieve the right result for the wrong reasons. Still we must admit, albeit ruefully, that the process can be entertaining.

ALEKHINE'S DEFENSE

Felixstowe, 1949

White	*Black*
FULLER	DERBY
1 P–K4	N–KB3
2 P–K5	N–Q4
3 P–QB4	N–N3
4 P–B5!?	. . . .

After this reckless-looking advance White's Pawns should turn out to be very weak. Actually the point never comes up.

4	N–Q4
5 N–QB3	N×N
6 QP×N	P–Q3
7 Q–N3!?	. . . .

White plays aggressively instead of preoccupying himself unduly with the fate of the advanced Pawns.

7	P×KP?

Black unwittingly involves himself in serious difficulties. Instead, he should develop with gain of time by playing 7 . . . N–B3!

Position after 7 . . . P×KP?

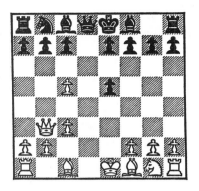

8 B–KN5!   **. . . .**

This sly move is a prelude to the mating threat 9 B–QB4, when . . . P–K3 will be impossible.

Here is a characteristic variation: 8 . . . P–KB3; 9 R–Q1, B–Q2 (on 9 . . . N–Q2; 10 B–QB4! is decisive); 10 Q×P, N–B3; 11 R×B!, K×R; 12 B–N5, P×B; 13 Q×Nch, K–B1; 14 B–R6ch and mate next move.

8 **. . . .**	**B–K3**
9 **Q×P**	**N–Q2**
10 **Castles**	**. . . .**

White threatens 11 P–B6 and wins.

10 **. . . .**	**Q–B1**
11 **Q–B6**	**P–QR3**

Otherwise 12 B–QR6 is too uncomfortable.

12 **N–B3**	**. . . .**

It will not do for Black to play 12 . . . P–B3 because of 13 Q×B, P×B; 14 N×NP, P–B3; 15 Q–B7ch, K–Q1; 16 N–K6 mate.

12 **. . . .**	**R–R2**
13 **N×P**	**P–B3**
14 **B–QB4!**	**Resigns**

Obviously 14 . . . P×B or 14 . . . P×N spells immediate ruin for Black after 15 B×B.

There remains 14 . . . B×B; 15 R×N, B—N4; 16 R—Q8 dbl ch! K×R; 17 N—B7 mate.

Black paid a heavy price for his faulty seventh move.

Variations on a Theme

HERE IS an even more attractive example of the double-Rook sacrifice than the ones we saw on pages 70 and 71. The absence of the defending Queen leads to a delightful Queen sacrifice.

CENTER COUNTER GAME

Budapest, 1934

(Simultaneous Exhibition)

White	Black
CANAL	AMATEUR
1 P–K4	P–Q4
2 P×P	Q×P
3 N–QB3	. . . .

The typical gain of time in this opening and in the Center Game (pages 21, 22 and 23).

3	Q–QR4
4 P–Q4	P–QB3

Excessive caution. It is a good idea to develop a piece, say 4 . . . N–KB3.

5 N–B3	B–N5
6 B–KB4	P–K3
7 P–KR3	B×N

One should not exchange a Bishop for a Knight so readily. Aside from that, Black brings the White Queen into active play.

8 Q×B	B–N5
9 B–K2	N–Q2
10 P–R3!	Castles?

Black carelessly relies on what he thinks is a fool-proof pin. It seems, superficially, that 11 P×B would be too expensive for White.

Position after 10 . . . Castles?

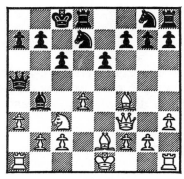

11 P×B!!	. . . .

Can it be that the master, playing many other games at the same time, has blundered?

11	Q×Rch
12 K—Q2!	Q×R
13 Q×Pch!!	. . . .

This is the sort of thing a master sees in a trice.

13	P×Q
14 B—QR6 mate	

Beautiful!

It is instructive to go back over the game to see how Black unwittingly forced White to go into this combination.

Multum in Parvo

THAT A KING can be quickly hounded to death by the hostile Queen in concert with other pieces, is hardly remarkable; but when several minor pieces can do the trick, the result is a miraculously beautiful mating process.

NIMZOVICH DEFENSE

Budapest, 1939

White	Black
AMATEUR	BARCZA
1 P–K4	N–QB3
2 P–Q4	P–Q4
3 P×P	. . . .

It may well be that 3 P–K5 is White's best chance to seize the initiative.

3	Q×P
4 N–KB3	B–N5

The safest reply to this is 5 B–K2, for an attempt on Black's part to win a Pawn would come to grief: 5 . . . B×N; 6 B×B, Q×QP??; 7 B×Nch winning Black's Queen.

5 N–B3?!	B×N!
6 N×Q	B×Q
7 N×BPch	K–Q2
8 N×R	B×P

Now the fate of the game turns on the question of whether White's Knight at Queen Rook 8 can escape.

| 9 B–KB4 | . . . . |

White hopes to play N–B7.

Position after 9 B–KB4

BLACK

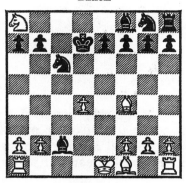

WHITE

| 9 .... | P–K4! |

A priceless gain of time. If White replies 10 B×P there follows 10 . . . B–N5ch; 11 K–K2, N×B; 12 P×N, N–K2; 13 R–B1, B–K5; 14 N–B7, B–B3 and White's advanced Knight is lost after all.

| 10 P×P | .... |

Now the diagonal of White's protective Bishop is broken.

10	B–N5ch
11 K–K2	KN–K2
12 P–K6ch	P×P
13 N–B7	....

After opening the critical diagonal, White has succeeded in moving out his stranded Knight. But Black has the last word after all.

| 13 .... | N–Q5ch |
| 14 K–K3 | N/K2–B4 mate |

White was so absorbed in solving the problem of his isolated Knight that he missed the point of Black's crafty arrangement of his pieces for an all-out assault on the White King.

The Laurels of Youth

EVERY GREAT MASTER, it seems, has one outstanding tournament success as a young man. This is the event that makes his genius known to the chess world. For Marshall, later destined to be U. S. Champion for almost 30 years, the important international tournament held at Paris in 1900 was such a contest. On that occasion he brushed aside all opposition as if his distinguished adversaries were so many Rook-odds players.

QUEEN'S GAMBIT DECLINED

Paris, 1900

White	Black
MARSHALL	BURN
1 P–Q4	P–Q4
2 P–QB4	P–K3
3 N–QB3	N–KB3
4 B–N5	B–K2
5 P–K3	Castles

Here or next move Black should play . . . QN–Q2. It is important, as we shall see, to have the Knight available for recapturing in the event that White plays B.×N.

6 N–B3	P–QN3
7 B–Q3	B–N2
8 P×P	P×P

Here 8 . . . N×P, leading to some simplification, would give Black an easier game.

9 B×N	B×B
10 P–KR4	. . . .

With the threat (or pseudothreat) of 11 B×Pch, K×B; 12 N–N5ch. This may not be sound, but the implications are menacing. Black's troubles stem from the fact that he lacks a protective Knight at his King Bishop 3 square.

10	P–N3

Black parries the threat—but at the cost of permitting White to open the King Rook file.

11 P–R5	. . . .

This cannot be answered by 11 . . . P–KN4 because of 12 P–R6! followed by 13 Q–B2 winning a Pawn.

11	R–K1
12 P×P	RP×P
13 Q–B2	B–N2

A reflex action to shield his King—but it is too late.

Position after 13 . . . B–N2

BLACK

WHITE

14 B×P!	. . . .

White denudes the Black King of Pawn protection.

14	P×B
15 Q×P	N–Q2
16 N–KN5	. . . .

White has two mating threats.

16	Q–B3

Black parries one of the threats (17 Q—B7 mate) but he is helpless against the other one.

17 **R—R8ch!**   **Resigns**

For 17 . . . K × R is answered by 18 Q—R7 mate. White has executed a dashing attack in a most attractive manner.

Knight Forks and (K)nightmares

THE KNIGHT FORK is the special dread of every inexperienced player. But even strong players can find themselves entangled in webs of Knight forks.

QUEEN'S GAMBIT DECLINED

New York, 1913

White	Black
MARSHALL	KLINE
1 P–Q4	P–Q4
2 P–QB4	P–K3
3 N–QB3	N–KB3
4 N–B3	B–K2
5 B–N5	QN–Q2
6 P–K3	Castles
7 R–B1	P–QN3

After this move Black runs the danger of incurring a weakness on the white squares. For this reason the modern masters prefer the more neutral 7 . . . P–B3.

8 P×P	P×P
9 Q–R4	. . . .

This move begins a policy of trying to exploit a weakness on the white squares on Black's Queen-side. It may well be that Black's most energetic course is to part with a Pawn for good counterplay: 9 . . . P–B4!; 10 Q–B6, R–N1; 11 N×P, N×N; 12 Q×N, B–N2 with a very promising game for Black.

9	B–N2
10 B–QR6!	B×B
11 Q×B	P–B3?

A timid move that leads to serious trouble in a surprisingly short time. The alternative 11 . . . P—B4 is much more energetic.

12 **Castles**		**N—K5**
13 **B×B**		**Q×B**
14 **Q—N7!**		**. . . .**

The winning move.

14 . . . .   **KR—B1**

Position after 14 . . . KR—B1

WHITE

15 **N×P!**   **Q—Q3**

Of course if 15 . . . P×N; 16 R×Rch and White is a Pawn and the Exchange ahead.

16 **R×P!!**   **Resigns**

Several neat points are involved here.

To begin with, if Black plays 16 . . . Q×N White wins the Black Queen with 17 R×Rch etc.

Or if Black plays 16 . . . Q×R White wins the Black Queen with 17 N—K7ch etc.

Finally, if Black tries 16 . . . R×R we get 17 Q× QRch, N—B1; 18 Q×R!, Q×Q; 19 N—K7ch and 20 N×Q; this leaves White a Rook ahead.

These delightful tactical turns all became possible as a result of White's terrific pressure on the weakened white squares.

Surprise!

TRYING TO ESCAPE from a disagreeable line of play, Black stumbles into disaster.

QUEEN'S GAMBIT DECLINED

Buenos Aires, 1952

White	Black
CASAS	PIAZZINI
1 P–Q4	P–Q4
2 P–QB4	P–K3
3 N–QB3	N–KB3
4 N–B3	B–K2
5 B–N5	QN–Q2
6 P–K3	Castles
7 Q–B2	P–B4
8 BP×P	N×P

The usual continuation is now 9 B×B, Q×B; 10 N×N, P×P; 11 P×P, N×P—whereby Black has freedom of action in return for an isolated Queen Pawn which may come under pressure from White's pieces.

| 9 N×N | . . . . |

Now it is still possible for Black to transpose into the previous note with 9 . . . P×N; 10 B×B, Q×B etc. Instead he varies.

| 9 . . . . | B×B |
| 10 P–KR4! | . . . . |

A successful attempt to entrap Black, who should resist sturdily with 10 . . . B–K2.

| 10 . . . . | Q–R4ch?? |

This plausible interpolation loses.

Position after 10 . . . Q–R4ch??

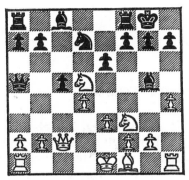

11 P–QN4!!   . . . .

Completely unexpected by Black. It is now too late for him to retreat his Queen, for then 12 P×B (threatening Q×RP mate) leaves White a piece ahead.

11 . . . .   **P×NP**

This looks like a clever resource, for after 12 P×B Black has 12 . . . P–N6 dis ch driving White's Queen off the critical diagonal. Then, after 13 Q–Q2 or 13 Q–B3, Black can safely answer 13 . . . Q×N and all's well.

This is as far as Black calculated. White, on the other hand, saw further ahead.

         12 Q×Pch!!   **K×Q**
         13 P×B dis ch   **K–N3**
         14 N–K7 mate

One of the greatest surprise combinations ever perpetrated on an unsuspecting opponent.

Strategy versus Tactics

To HAVE A PLAN is a good thing, but planning must always take account of salient details. Black's 12 . . . P×B? is based on an admirable strategical idea (reducing the scope of White's Knights). But all this is turned topsy-turvy by White's scintillating sacrificial combination.

QUEEN'S GAMBIT DECLINED

New York, 1929

White	*Black*
HANAUER	BARTHA
1 P–Q4	N–KB3
2 N–KB3	P–K3
3 P–B4	P–Q4
4 B–N5	QN–Q2
5 P–K3	B–K2
6 QN–Q2	. . . .

Varying from the more customary N–B3. At Queen 2 the Knight has less scope, though there are prospects of its reaching King 5 via Queen Bishop 4.

6	Castles
7 B–Q3	P–QR3

In positions of this kind, . . . P–B4 is Black's best equalizing move.

8 Castles	P–B4
9 Q–K2	R–K1

This serves no useful purpose and at the same time it

has the drawback of weakening the protection of Black's King Bishop Pawn.

10 KR–Q1	BP×P
11 KP×P	P×P

In his haste to isolate White's Queen Pawn Black brings White's Queen Knight into powerful play.

12 N×P	P–QN4
13 N/B4–K5	B–N2
14 B×N	P×B?

This plausible move—played to keep White's Knights out of King 5—is a decisive mistake.

Position after 14 . . . P×B?

BLACK

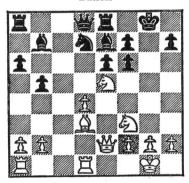

WHITE

15 N×P!!	. . . .

A bombshell.

15	K×N
16 N–K5ch!!	. . . .

Another beautiful move which leaves Black little choice, for if 16 . . . K–B1 or 16 . . . K–N1; 17 Q–R5 wins; while on 16 . . . K–N2; 17 Q–N4ch is decisive.

16	P×N

On 16 . . . N×N White wins neatly by 17 Q–R5ch, N–N3; 18 Q×RPch etc.

17 Q–R5ch	K–N2
18 Q×RPch	K–B1
19 Q–R6ch	. . . .

In the heat of the battle White overlooks that 19 B—N6! leaves Black helpless against the impending Q—B7 mate or Q—R8 mate.

19	K—N1
20 B—R7ch	Resigns

The only choice left to Black is how he wants to be mated: 20 . . . K—B2; 21 Q—N6ch, K—B1; 22 Q—N8 mate, or 20 . . . K—R1; 21 B—N6 dis ch, K—N1; 22 Q—R7ch and mate next move.

Black's suicidal combination of 9 . . . R—K1 and 14 . . . P×B laid his King-side bare to a devastating attack.

Hitting 'em Where They Ain't

ONE OF THE WONDERS OF CHESS is the seemingly miraculous way that an attack ostensibly aimed at the Queenside suddenly turns into an attack on the other wing. The explanation? Superior mobility.

QUEEN'S GAMBIT DECLINED

New York, 1926

White	*Black*
E. LASKER	WINKELMAN
1 N–KB3	N–KB3
2 P–Q4	P–Q4
3 P–B4	P–K3
4 B–N5	QN–Q2
5 P–K3	B–K2
6 N–B3	Castles
7 B–Q3	P–QR3

Good enough, although here and on the next two moves . . . P–B4 is the natural way to equalize.

| 8 N–K5!? | P×P |
| 9 N×QBP | P–QN4?? |

This strategical blunder allows White's wandering Knight to make dangerous inroads into Black's position.

10 N–R5!	P–B4
11 N–B6	Q–K1
12 Q–B3!	. . . .

Position after 12 Q—B3!

BLACK

WHITE

An intolerable situation for Black. White threatens to win a Rook by 13 N×Bch and 14 Q×R.

| 12 . . . . | N—N3 |

Protecting the menaced Rook. On 12 . . . B—N2? the reply 13 N×Bch would win a piece.

| 13 N—K4! | . . . . |

The first point of this exceedingly powerful stroke is that 13 . . . Q×N is answered by 14 N×Nch winning the Black Queen.

Even more interesting is the alternative 13 . . . B—N2; 14 N×Bch, Q×N; 15 N×Nch, P×N; 16 Q—R5 winning Black's Queen as 16 . . . P—B4 is the only way to stop mate.

| 13 . . . . | KN—Q4 |

Losing quickly, but 13 . . . N×N; 14 N×Bch, K—R1; 15 B×N leaves Black hopelessly behind in material.

| 14 N×Bch | N×N |
| 15 N—B6ch!! | Resigns |

A very fine finish. The concluding moves might have been: 15 ... P×N; 16 B×Pch!, K×B; 17 Q–R5ch, K–N2; 18 Q–R6ch, K–N1; 19 B×P, N–N3; 20 Q–N7 mate.

Black's lapse on move 9 allowed White's forces to penetrate rapidly, smashing down Black's flimsy defense in the process.

Smash-up

BLACK'S LACKLUSTER OPENING leaves him without resources against White's energetic middle-game attack. It is difficult for the amateur to realize the close-knit connection between these two phases.

QUEEN'S GAMBIT DECLINED

New York State Championship, 1910

White	Black
CAPABLANCA	JAFFE
1 P—Q4	P—Q4
2 N—KB3	N—KB3
3 P—K3	P—B3
4 P—B4	P—K3

Black assures his forces more freedom of action by playing 4 . . . B—B4.

5 N—B3	QN—Q2
6 B—Q3	B—Q3
7 Castles	Castles
8 P—K4	P×KP
9 N×P	N×N
10 B×N	N—B3
11 B—B2	. . . .

With a view to 12 Q—Q3 and 13 B—N5, threatening 14 B×N and 15 Q×P mate.

11	P—KR3

Black meets the threat but weakens his King-side.

12 P—QN3	P—QN3
13 B—N2	B—N2
14 Q—Q3	. . . .

A new threat: 15 P–Q5 menacing 16 B×N and 17 Q–R7 mate.

14	**P–N3**

Again stopping the threat but weakening the castled position.

15 **QR–K1!**	. . . .

Now the threat of R×P! is in the air.

15	**N–R4**
16 **B–B1!**	**K–N2**

But not 16 . . . N–B5; 17 B×N, B×B; 18 R×P!, P×R; 19 Q×Pch and mate next move. The weakening of Black's King-side is beginning to tell.

Position after 16 . . . K–N2

BLACK

WHITE

17 **R×P!**	**N–B3**

Naturally Black avoids 17 . . . P×R; 18 Q×Pch, K–R1; 19 Q–R7 mate.

18 **N–K5!**	**P–B4**

After 18 . . . P×R; 19 Q×Pch, K–R1; 20 Q×Pch,

K–N1; 21 Q–N6ch, K–R1; 22 R–K1 White wins easily
by bringing his remaining Rook to the third rank.

| 19 B×Pch! | K×B |
| 20 N×BPch! | Resigns |

For after 20 . . . R×N White has 21 Q×P mate.
Note that White removed all of Black's King-side Pawns
by sacrifices.

Sweet Are the Uses of Mobility

IN CHESS, mobility is often the secret of success. The following game is an admirable instance of the principle that the future belongs to the player who has superior mobility.

QUEEN'S GAMBIT DECLINED

(in effect)
Sopron, 1934

White	Black
SPIELMANN	FUSS
1 P–Q4	N–KB3
2 N–KB3	P–K3
3 P–B4	B–N5ch
4 QN–Q2	N–K5
5 P–K3	N×N
6 B×N	B×Bch
7 Q×B	P–Q4
8 R–B1	P–QB3

Black has followed standard procedure in striving to relieve his cramped position by several simplifying exchanges. White still retains a noticeably freer game, however.

9 B–Q3	N–Q2
10 Castles	Castles
11 P–K4!	• • • •

White opens up the game still more, giving his pieces even greater maneuvering space.

11	P×KP
12 B×P	N—B3
13 B—N1	P—QN3
14 Q—B4	B—N2
15 N—K5	. . . .

Move by move White enhances the aggressive character of his position. Black should now open his Bishop's diagonal, and at the same time obtain more play in the center, by playing . . . P—B4.

15	Q—B2?

An unfortunate position for the Black Queen, as we shall see.

16 R—B3!	. . . .

The Rook's action along the third rank can be very powerful, as in this typical variation: 16 . . . QR—B1; 17 R—KN3, K—R1; 18 R×P!!, K×R; 19 Q—N5ch, K—R1; 20 Q×Nch, K—N1; 21 R—K1!, KR—Q1; 22 B×Pch!, K—B1 (if 22 . . . K×B; 23 R—K3 carries the decisive menace of R—KR3ch); 23 N—N6ch, K—K1; 24 R×Pch! and Black is soon mated.

16	N—R4

Position after 16 . . . N—R4

BLACK

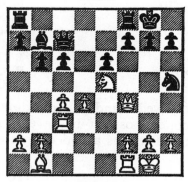

WHITE

17 B×Pch!   . . . .

Black cannot turn down the Bishop with 17 . . . K–R1?? for then 18 N–N6ch wins Black's Queen. This is our first intimation that the unprotected position of the Black Queen is unfortunate.

17	K×B
18 R–KR3	K–N1

A pretty variation here is 18 . . . P–N3; 19 N×NP, Q×Q (what else); 20 N×Q and White recovers the piece with two Pawns to the good.

19 R×N	P–B3
20 R–R8ch!	Resigns

White is still harping on the same old theme (if 20 . . . K×R; 21 N–N6ch wins the Black Queen). For a concrete example of superior mobility, note how White's 11 P–K4! opened up the third rank for his Rooks.

The Two Bishops

IN THE HANDS OF A MASTER, two efficiently cooperating Bishops make a fearsome weapon.

QNEEN'S GAMBIT

Nuremberg, 1896

White	Black
JANOWSKI	SCHALLOPP
1 P–Q4	P–Q4
2 P–QB4	P×P
3 N–KB3	P–QB4
4 P–K3	P×P
5 P×P	B–N5?

The more conservative . . . N–KB3 was in order.

| 6 B×P | . . . . |

White threatens 7 B×Pch!, K×B; 8 N–K5ch or 8 N–N5ch with a winning position.

| 6 . . . . | P–K3 |
| 7 Q–R4ch! | . . . . |

White alertly exploits the absence of Black's Queen Bishop from home base. Thus if Black replies 7 . . . N–Q2 there follows 8 N–K5, KN–B3; 9 B–KN5! (threatening N × B), B–KB4; 10 N × N, Q × N; 11 B–N5 winning the Black Queen.

| 7 . . . . | N–QB3 |
| 8 N–K5 | Q×P |

In view of White's double attack on Knight and Bishop, Black has no choice.

9 N×N	Q–K5ch
10 B–K3	P×N

He avoids 10 . . . Q×N??; 11 B–QN5 winning the Queen.

11 N–B3	Q×P

The only way to continue his protection of the Queen Bishop Pawn. And meanwhile he threatens . . . Q×Rch.

Position after 11 . . . Q×P

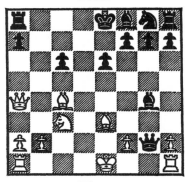

12 B–Q5!!	. . . .

This beautiful move drives off Black's Queen from the defense.

12	KP×B
13 Q×BPch	K–Q1

Likewise after 13 . . . K–K2; 14 N×Pch, K–Q1; 15 Q×Rch Black can resign.

14 Q×Rch	K–Q2
15 Q–N7ch	K–K3
16 Q–B6ch	B–Q3
17 B–B4!!	Resigns

For after 17 . . . Q×Rch; 18 K—Q2, Q×R; 19 Q×ᷭ
Bch White has a quick mate: 19 . . . K—B4; 20 Q—
K5ch, K—N3; 21 Q—KN5 mate.

Black opened up the position prematurely, weakened his Queen-side and let his Queen be driven away. Result: disaster.

"I Dare You!"

IN CHESS, as in international relations, it is a serious matter when a bluff is called. Here Black challenges his opponent to sacrifice a Rook, never dreaming that White will accept the challenge. The moral: look before you challenge.

QUEEN'S GAMBIT

U. S. Championship Preliminaries, 1940

White	Black
REINFELD	BATTELL
1 N–KB3	P–Q4
2 P–Q4	N–KB3
3 P–B4	P×P
4 P–K3	P–B4
5 B×P	P×P
6 P×P	Q–B2
7 Q–N3	B–K3??

The orthodox . . . P–K3 was preferable.

Position after 7 . . . B—K3??

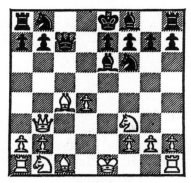

8 B×B!!	Q×Bch

Black cannot draw back now, for after 8 . . . P×B; 9 N—B3 the weakness of his Pawn on King 3 would be fatal.

9 K—K2	Q×R
10 B×Pch	. . . .

White has a quicker and prettier win with 10 Q×P!!, P×B; 11 Q—B8ch, K—B2; 12 N—K5ch, K—N1; 13 Q×P mate.

10	K—Q1

The alternative 10 . . . K—Q2; 11 Q×Pch is equally hopeless for Black.

11 Q×P	Q—QB8
12 Q×R!	Q×Pch
13 QN—Q2	. . . .

White sees that Black must not play 13 . . . Q×R because of 14 Q×Nch, K—Q2; 15 N—K5 mate.

13	N—K5
14 Q×N/K4	Q×R
15 Q—Q5ch	K—B2
16 Q—B5ch	K—Q1

An amusing alternative would be 16 . . . K—N2; 17 B—Q5ch and Black's game is in the last throes.

17 B—K6	Resigns

For after 17 . . . N–Q2; 18 Q–B6, N–N3; 19 N–
K5 Black is helpless against the coming 20 N–B7 mate.
Black's challenge proved faulty because of his lack of
development.

Is This a System?

YEARS AGO the famous Belgian master Edgard Colle refurbished a nondescript Queen's Pawn opening and transformed it into a powerful attacking weapon. So impressive were his successes that the opening took on the name of Colle System. But there is an ebb and flow in such processes and eventually the "system" lost its appeal.

COLLE SYSTEM

Scarborough, 1928

White	*Black*
COLLE	SCHUBERT
1 P–Q4	P–Q4
2 N–KB3	N–KB3
3 P–K3	P–K3

As White's next move forms the basis of his attacking possibilities, the indicated move here is 3 . . . B–B4.

4 B–Q3	P–B4
5 P–B3	QN–Q2
6 QN–Q2	P×P

This feeble move opens the King file for White's Rooks as well as the diagonal of his Queen Bishop. It also provides him with an opportunity to post his King Knight powerfully at King 5.

7 KP×P	B–Q3
8 Castles	Castles
9 R–K1	Q–B2
10 Q–K2	. . . .

White has won the fight centering around his posting a Knight at King 5.

10	R–K1
11 N–K5	N–B1
12 N/Q2–B3	N/B3–Q2
13 N–N5!	....

While Black retreats, White steadily makes headway.

Position after 13 N–N5!

BLACK

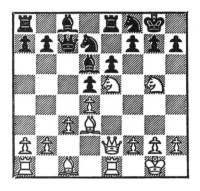

WHITE

13 . . . .   P–B3

Apparently winning a piece. But White has seen much further ahead.

14 Q–R5!   . . . .

On 14 . . . P × N/N4 White plans 15 B × Pch!, N × B; 16 Q–B7ch, K–R1; 17 N–N6 mate.

And on 14 . . . P × N/K4 the continuation would be 15 B × Pch, N × B; 16 Q × Nch, K–B1; 17 Q–R8ch, K–K2; 18 Q × Pch with an overwhelming attack.

| 14 . . . . | P–KN3 |
| 15 N × NP! | . . . . |

The reply 15 . . . RP × N would be refuted by 16 B × P, P × N; 17 B–B7ch!, K–N2; 18 B × R with an easy win for White.

| 15 . . . . | BP × N |
| 16 N × N | N–B3 |

191

If 16 . . . R×N; 17 Q×RP mate. If 16 . . . K×N; 17 Q–R6ch, K–K2; 18 B×NPch and wins.

| 17 Q×NPch | Q–N2 |
| 18 N×RP! | Resigns |

If Black plays 18 . . . Q×Q White replies 19 N×Q with three Pawns to the good. An amusing alternative is 18 . . . N×N; 19 B×Nch, K×B; 20 Q–R5ch picking up the loose Rook. White refuted Black's faulty play in attractive style.

The Looming Long Diagonal

ONE OF THE GREAT ACHIEVEMENTS of modern masters is the demonstration of a Bishop's power on a long diagonal. The following game is a good example.

NIMZOINDIAN DEFENSE

Scarborough, 1930

White	*Black*
WINTER	COLLE
1 P–Q4	N–KB3
2 P–QB4	P–K3
3 N–QB3	B–N5

The basic idea of this defense is Black's projected control of the center by pieces rather than by center Pawns. In this sense, 3 . . . B–N5 is a substitute for 3 . . . P–Q4.

4 Q–N3	P–B4
5 P×P	N–B3
6 N–B3	N–K5
7 B–Q2	N×QBP
8 Q–B2	P–B4

In line with the previous note, Black controls the King 5 square with . . . P–B4 rather than with . . . P–Q4.

9 P–K3	Castles
10 P–QR3	B×N
11 B×B	. . . .

Now White has two Bishops against Bishop and Knight.

193

Ordinarily this is an advantage, but in the sequel we find that White's Bishops have little scope.

11	. . . .	P–QN3
12	B–K2	B–N2

This Bishop, on the other hand, is destined to decide the game in Black's favor.

13	Castles(K)	R–B1
14	KR–Q1	Q–K2
15	P–QN4	N–K5
16	B–K1	R–B3!

An ominous development. The Rook is to go to King Knight 3, from where it will cooperate with the long-range Bishop in pressure against White's King Knight 2 square.

17	N–Q4?	. . . .

This extends the range of Black's Bishop and is therefore questionable. Instead, 17 B–B1 offered better defensive prospects, though its passive character is no recommendation.

17	. . . .	R–N3!

Black's formation is becoming menacing. For example, on 18 P–B3 Black wins with 18 . . . Q–N4!

18	B–B1	N–N4!

And now Black threatens to win with 19 . . . N×N; 20 P×N, N–B6ch; 21 K–R1, Q–R5! (similar to the actual play).

19	K–R1	N×N
20	P×N	. . . .

Position after 20 P×N

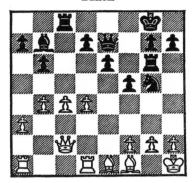

20 . . . .   N—B6!!
Resigns

White is pathetically helpless. If he tries 21 P–Q5 (to shut off the terrible Bishop), Black wins with 21 . . . Q–R5 (threatens mate); 22 P×N, Q–N4 followed by mate—or 22 P–R3, Q×RPch!; 23 P×Q, R–N8 mate.

Too Much of a Good Thing

SOME PLAYERS think that repeated exchanges lead automatically to a draw. It is a dangerous delusion.

QUEEN'S INDIAN DEFENSE

Liege, 1953

White	Black
SOULTANBEIEFF	DUBYNA
1 P–Q4	N–KB3
2 P–QB4	P–K3
3 N–KB3	P–QN3
4 P–K3	. . . .

There is more punch in this quiet move than one might suppose.

4	B–N2
5 B–Q3	B–K5
6 N–B3	B–N5

Black tries to control the center with his pieces. This policy is destined to fail for tactical reasons.

7 Q–B2	. . . .

White loses a move in order to clear the situation.

7	B×B
8 Q×B	P–Q4

To prevent P–K4.

9 P×P	. . . .

196

Now 9 . . . P×P? is answered by 10 Q—N5ch and White wins a piece.

9	N×P
10 Castles	N×N
11 P×N	B—K2
12 N—K5	. . . .

Despite the exchanges—or perhaps because of them —White retains the initiative.

12	Castles
13 P—KB4	P—QB4
14 P—B5	KP×P
15 Q×P	. . . .

Position after 15 Q×P

BLACK

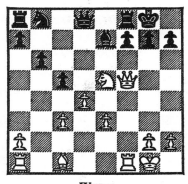

WHITE

Now Black finds that the uncomfortable threat of 16 N×P, Q—K1; 17 Q—Q5! is not so easy to answer.

15 . . . .   Q—Q4?

This loses. His best chance was 15 . . . B—B3.

16 N—N6!   Q—N2

Naturally he cannot capture the Knight, and if 16 . . . Q×Q; 17 N×Bch wins a piece.

17 Q—Q5!   N—B3

Or 17 . . . Q×Q; 18 N×Bch etc.

18 Q×N!   Resigns

Still the same story: 18 . . . Q×Q; 19 N×Bch and 20 N×Q. An elegant finish.

Fun's Fun

THIS LIGHT-HEARTED GAME makes no pretensions to being a full-blown masterpiece. For all that, it's great fun to follow and by no means lacking in instructive points.

KING'S INDIAN DEFENSE

Ostend, 1907

White	Black
MARSHALL	BURN
1 P–Q4	N–KB3
2 N–KB3	P–Q3
3 B–B4	QN–Q2
4 P–K3	P–KN3
5 B–Q3	B–N2
6 QN–Q2	Castles
7 P–KR4!?	....

"Nowadays," Marshall commented many years later, "this move would be regarded with horror because of its antipositional character; but I was determined to play for attack at all costs."

7	R–K1
8 P–R5!?	....

Naïve or not, White is certainly consistent. Incidentally, 8 . . . P–K4 does not win a piece because of 9 B–KN5 (9 . . . P–K5?; 10 N×P etc.).

8	N×P

Playable, though it certainly tempts fate.

9 R×N!?	....

This is no time to haggle.

| 9 .... | P×R |
| 10 B×Pch!? | .... |

Position after 10 B × Pch!?

BLACK

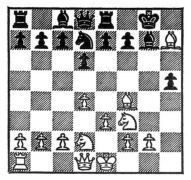

WHITE

| 10 .... | K×B? |

After this Black is lost. On the other hand, it is not clear how White would have cashed in on his investment after 10 . . . K–B1!

| 11 N–N5ch | K–N3 |

The seemingly safer 11 . . . K–N1? would lose even more rapidly after 12 Q × P, N–B3; 13 Q × Pch, K–R1; 14 Castles, whereupon 15 R–R1ch comes up like thunder.

| 12 N/Q2–B3 | .... |

Threatening to win at once with 13 Q–Q3ch, P–KB4; 14 N–R4ch etc.

| 12 .... | P–K4 |
| 13 N–R4ch | K–B3 |

Or 13 . . . K–R3; 14 N × P dbl ch winning the Queen.

| 14 N–R7ch | K–K2 |
| 15 N–B5ch | .... |

The Knights are diabolically active.

15	K–K3
16 N×Bch	K–K2
17 N–B5ch	K–K3

Black's King is driven into a mating net.

18	P—Q5ch	K×N
19	Q×Pch	K—K5
20	Castles	Resigns

The only way to meet the threat of 21 P—B3 mate is 20 . . . P×B; but then comes 21 R—Q4 mate. Vastly entertaining.

Premature Suicide

SHORT OF ACTUAL BLUNDERS, lack of faith in one's position is the chief cause of defeat. To be sure, it is easy to recommend faith and not so easy to practice it.

KING'S INDIAN DEFENSE

London, 1927

White	Black
PALAU	TE KOLSTE
1 N–KB3	N–KB3
2 P–Q4	P–KN3
3 N–B3	P–Q4
4 B–B4	N–R4

This is open to the general objection to repeated moves of the same piece in the opening. The objection is particularly in order when Black is the one who is wasting time. Instead, 4 . . . P–B3 or 4 . . . B–N2 should have been played.

5 B–K5!   . . . .

This, on the other hand, is not waste of time as it provokes a weakness in Black's game which may turn out to be significant later on.

5	P–KB3
6 B–N3	N×B
7 RP×N	. . . .

White has gained the open King Rook file as a possible base of operations.

7		B–N2
8 P–K3		P–B3
9 B–Q3		P–K4?

Black doesn't realize what he is heading into. Even now it was relatively better to castle.

Position after 9 . . . P–K4?

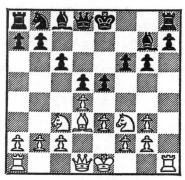

10 R×P!		. . . .

White can answer 10 . . . R×R with 11 B×Pch, coming out two Pawns to the good.

10		K–B2?

Feeble. The most interesting try is 10 . . . P–K5, though it leaves White with a complicated win: 11 R×B, P×B (threatening a Rook check); 12 Q×P, B–B4 (the only move if he wants to fight on); 13 P–K4, K–B1 (if 13 . . . P×P; 14 Q–B4! wins); 14 P×B, R–R8ch; 15 K–Q2, R×R; 16 R–R7! (threatens R–R8ch), K–N1; 17 P×P and White wins quickly.

11 B×Pch!!		. . . .

The real fireworks.

11		K×B
12 N×Pch!!		. . . .

Very fine. On 12 . . . K×R there follows 13 Q–

R5ch, K–N1 forced; 14 Q–B7ch, K–R2; 15 Castles with mate to come.

12	**P×N**
13 Q–R5ch	**K–B3**
14 Q×Pch	**K–B2**

Or 14 . . . K–N3; 15 Q×Bch, K–B4; 16 P–KN4ch, K–K3; 17 Q–K5 mate.

15 Q×Bch	**Resigns**

If 15 . . . K–K1; 16 Q–KB7 mate or if 15 . . . K–K3; 16 Q–K5 mate. An elegant attack.

Man's Undying Spirit

MORE AND MORE we hear complaints that the ever en-croaching advance of technique is stifling creative effort. In the field of chess, such complaints have been rife for decades. Yet every now and then we see games like this one, to prove to us that it is not an easy thing to bottle the imp of adventurousness.

KING'S INDIAN DEFENSE

Uppsala, 1958

White	Black
SZUKSZTA	TAL
1 P–Q4	N–KB3
2 P–QB4	P–KN3
3 N–QB3	B–N2
4 P–K4	P–Q3

Black's game can easily become seriously cramped un-less he is prepared to take vigorous measures.

5 P–B3	Castles
6 B–K3	P–K4
7 KN–K2	P–B3

White can now maintain a fine game with Q–Q2 fol-lowed by Castles.

8 Q–N3?	. . . .

This foolhardy move is played to restrain Black from freeing his game with . . . P–Q4.

8	P×P
9 N×P	P–Q4!

Black thumbs his nose at White's policy of restraint.

| 10 | BP×P | P×P |
| 11 | P×P | R—K1! |

The first point of Black's Pawn sacrifice. But the best is yet to be.

| 12 | K—B2 | •••• |

Position after 12 K—B2

BLACK

WHITE

| 12 | •••• | N—B3‼ |

Beautiful play.

| 13 | P×N | R×B! |

This is what Black has been leading up to.

It is clear that 14 K×R will not do because of 14 . . . B—R3ch; 15 P—B4, B×Pch with a winning attack for Black.

After 14 P×P, Q×N! the continuation might be 15 P×B/Qch (not 15 P×R/Q, R—K1 dis ch; 16 K—N3, N—R4 mate), R×Q.

Now Black should win, as may be seen from the following variations: 16 Q—R4, R×P dbl ch!; 17 K×R,

R × Nch! winning White's Queen—or 16 K–N3, N–R4ch;
17 K–R3, Q–Q2ch with mate in the offing.

14 R–Q1	N–N5ch!
15 P×N	B×N
16 R×B	Q×R
17 Q–Q5	R–K7 dbl ch!!

An exquisite resource.

18 K×R	B×Pch
19 K–K1	R–K1ch
20 B–K2	R×Bch
Resigns	

White loses his Queen. This was a rapid-transit game—
a matter of a few minutes.

The Vulnerable Queen?

ONE OF THE IMPORTANT PRINCIPLES of opening play is not to play out the Queen at an early stage when she is sure to be harried by the attacks of hostile pieces. When Black applies the rule unthinkingly, he comes a cropper.

GRUENFELD DEFENSE

Amsterdam, 1940

White	*Black*
KMOCH	PRINS
1 P–Q4	N–KB3
2 P–QB4	P–KN3
3 N–QB3	P–Q4
4 N–B3	B–N2
5 Q–N3	P×P
6 Q×BP	. . . .

White, we see, has played out his Queen at a very early stage.

6	Castles
7 P–K4	P–N3
8 P–K5	B–K3

Black drives off the Queen in order to plant his King Knight unassailably at Queen 4. But White refuses to be driven.

Position after 8 B—K3

BLACK

WHITE

9 P×N!	....

White will get more than enough material for his Queen.

9	B×Q
10 P×B	K×P

Even worse for Black is 10 . . . B×B; 11 P×R/Qch and White winds up with Rook, Bishop and Knight for Queen and Pawn—a winning material advantage.

11 B×B	N—B3
12 B—K3	N—N5

White has some material advantage and he gains a lot of time, and a valuable open file, from Black's wasteful maneuver with his remaining Knight.

13 Castles(K)	N—B7
14 QR—Q1	N×B
15 P×N	P—QB4
16 N—KN5!	....

This sudden attack menaces 17 R×Pch!, R×R; 18 N—K6ch winning Black's Queen.

16	P—K3

What to do? On 16 . . . Q—K1 a likely continuation

is 17 P×P, P×P; 18 B–N5, Q–B1; 19 R–Q7 and the pressure becomes intolerable.

17 R×Pch! **Resigns**

Black does not wait for 17 . . . K–R3; 18 R×RPch!, K×N; 19 P–KR4ch, K–N5; 20 B–K2ch, K–N6; 21 N–K4 mate. Note the telling contrast between White's alert play and Black's sluggish, ill-timed moves.

Getting Mated in Five Moves

CAN SUCH THINGS BE? They can indeed, and I saw this game played in less time than it takes to describe.

BUDAPEST DEFENSE

Philadelphia, 1936

White	Black
ARNOLD	HANAUER
1 P–Q4	N–KB3
2 P–QB4	P–K4

A speculative Pawn offer. After 3 P × P, N–N5 Black expects to regain the proffered Pawn or at least to gain time to speed his development.

3 P–Q5?	. . . .

Pointless loss of time. Preferable is 3 P × P, N–N5; 4 P–K4, whereby White returns the extra Pawn at once and gains time to bring out his pieces.

3	B–B4

Taking stock at this point we find that Black has developed two pieces, while White has confined himself to Pawn moves.

4 B–N5?	. . . .

At last a developing move, but a most unsuitable one. Instead, 4 N–QB3 was called for.

Position after 4 B–N5?

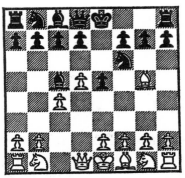

4 . . . .   **N–K5!**

Already threatening mate—and attacking White's developed Bishop as well.

5 B×Q??   . . . .

White's "best" was 5 B–K3, although after 5 . . . B×B; 6 P×B, Q–R5ch Black would obviously have had a winning advantage.

5 . . . .   **B×P mate**

Black's keen concentration on development is in glaring contrast to White's failure to get effective work out of his pieces.

The New and the Old

IT IS ONE OF THE FEATURES of the new-fangled catch-as-can openings that considerable time generally elapses before the players come to grips. The ponderous maneuvering often rules out tricky tactics in the early stages. Here we have a heart-warming exception.

CATALAN OPENING

Buxton, 1950

White	Black
VEITCH	PENROSE
1 P–Q4	N–KB3
2 P–QB4	P–K3
3 N–KB3	P–Q4
4 P–KN3	. . . .

"Old-fashioned" moves such as 4 B–N5 or 4 N–B3 would leave us in the realm of the Queen's Gambit Declined.

4	P×P
5 QN–Q2	P–B4

Now White should simply continue 6 N×P with an excellent game. For example, after 6 . . . P×P; 7 Q×P he would have an appreciable lead in development—not to mention the splendid prospects for his King Bishop on the long diagonal after B–N2 in due course.

6 P×P	B×P

White has neglected his own development and helped Black's King Bishop to an effective diagonal. There seems

nothing better available for White now than 7 Q–R4ch,
with 8 Q×BP to follow.

    7 B–N2??   • • • •

Who would suspect that this plausible-looking developing move would lead to disaster?

Position after 7 B–N2??

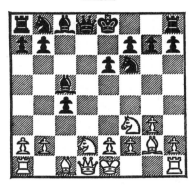

    7 • • • •   **B×Pch!!**

The proverbial bolt from the blue.

If White declines the Bishop with 8 K–B1 Black wins
with surprising suddenness by playing 8 . . . N–N5!
He then threatens to win the White Queen with . . .
N–K6ch. Against this terrifying threat White is curiously
helpless, for example 9 Q–R4ch, B–Q2; 10 Q×BP,
N–K6ch winning the Black Queen.

Even more interesting is 9 Q–R4ch, B–Q2; 10 Q–R3,
N–QR3; 11 N×P, B–N4 and Black wins.

    8 K×B   **N–N5ch**
    9 K–K1   • • • •

The gloomy alternatives are very clean cut. On 9 K–B1
Black wins the White Queen with 9 . . . N–K6ch. And
on 9 K–N1, Black has 9 . . . Q–N3ch with mate in a
few moves to follow.

    9 • • • •   **N–K6**
    Resigns

White cannot save his Queen: 10 Q–R4ch, B–Q2! and now on 11 Q–N4 or 11 Q–R3 Black forks King and Queen with 11 . . . N–B7ch. Black's pieces co-operated beautifully.

Double Take

BLACK'S PAWN PLAY in the center looks plausible until we see that he has overreached himself. After two exchanges it suddenly turns out that Black has a lost game.

ENGLISH OPENING

New York, 1938

White	*Black*
MARSHALL	McCORMICK
1 P–QB4	P–K4
2 N–QB3	P–KB4
3 N–B3	N–QB3
4 P–Q4	P–K5
5 N–Q2	N–B3

Perhaps Black should have tried 5 . . . N×P; 6 N/Q2×P, N–K3.

6 P–K3	P–Q4?

And here 6 . . . B–N5 offers better chances.

7 P×P	. . . .

Position after 7 P×P

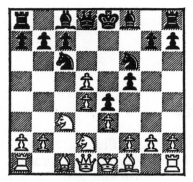

7 . . . .   N—QN5

Black is startled to discover that things are not quite what they seem.

Thus, if he plays 7 . . . KN×P White wins a Pawn with 8 N/Q2×P! On 8 . . . P×N there follows 9 Q—R5ch and White comfortably regains the piece. Similarly, after 8 . . . B—N5 White maintains his extra material with 9 B—Q2!

8 B—B4	N/N5×QP
9 N×N	N×N
10 N×P	. . . .

Still the same old song: if 10 . . . P×N; 11 Q—R5ch leaves White a Pawn ahead.

10	N×P?
11 B×N	P×N
12 Q—R5ch	Resigns

For on 12 . . . P—KN3 White wins with 13 Q—K5ch. Or 12 . . . K—Q2; 13 Q—Q5ch!, B—Q3; 14 Q—KB5ch! and it is mate next move. It is fascinating to study the way that the collapse of Black's center Pawns led to a general disaster.

Good or Bad?

THERE ARE TRAPS AND TRAPS. Some work splendidly if
the opponent succumbs. Others recoil badly if they are
avoided. Black's trap in the following game is a good one,
as it promises optimum results with minimum risk.

ENGLISH OPENING

London, 1939

White	*Black*
CRADDOCK	MIESES
1 P–QB4	P–K4
2 N–QB3	N–QB3
3 P–KN3	N–B3
4 B–N2	B–N5
5 P–K3	. . . .

White makes room for his King Knight at King 2 as
he does not want to block his King Bishop's diagonal.
However, he thereby weakens his white squares. This
doesn't matter as long as his King Bishop remains on the
board.

5	P–Q3
6 KN–K2	B–N5
7 Q–N3	. . . .

White threatens to win a piece with B × Nch.

7	QR–N1!

Black parries the threat, for after 8 B × Nch, P × B his
King Bishop will be protected.

8 N–Q5	B–QB4
9 N×Nch	Q×N!

217

Setting an exceptionally deep trap.

Position after 9 . . . Q×N!

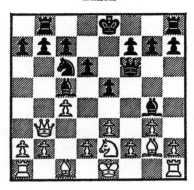

10 B×Nch?	P×B!
11 Q×Rch?	. . . .

Like Oscar Wilde, White can resist everything but temptation. As we know from earlier games, there is usually a heavy price tag on these two-Rook captures.

11	K–Q2
12 Q×R	. . . .

In the event of 12 Q–N3 (intending Q–Q1) Black has the same winning reply.

12	Q–B6!

Threatening 13 . . . Q×N mate as well as 13 . . . Q×Rch and mate the following move. How sorely the absence of White's white-squared Bishop is felt!

13 K–Q1	. . . .

No balm in Gilead. If White Castles, the reply 13 . . . B–KR6 forces mate. Similarly, on 13 K–B1 there follows 13 . . . Q×Nch; 14 K–N1, B–KR6, finis.

13	Q×Nch
14 K–B2	Q×BPch
15 K–N1	Q–Q6 mate

Very neat. Black must have had all this in mind when he played 7 . . . QR–N1!

218

The Queen Is In the Way

THE FINAL COMBINATION HERE has a curious motif: in order to force mate, White has to get his Queen out of the way. So a Queen sacrifice paves the way to victory.

BIRD'S OPENING

Munich, 1915

White	*Black*
TARRASCH	SATZINGER
1 P–KB4	P–K3
2 N–KB3	P–Q4
3 P–K3	P–QB4
4 P–QN3	B–K2
5 B–N2	B–B3

The idea of contesting the long diagonal is not bad but it leads to unforeseen consequences.

6 N–K5	B×N

Since Black changes his mind in midstream, he might just as well have played . . . N–K2 or . . . N–Q2 with fair prospects.

7 P×B!	. . . .

This allows Black to win a Pawn by 7 . . . Q–R5ch; 8 P–N3, Q–K5; 9 R–N1, P–Q5; 10 N–R3, Q×KP.

However, on further study of the position we find that White can regain the Pawn favorably with 11 N–B4, Q–B3; 12 P×P, P×P; 13 Q–N4, N–B3; 14 B–N2,

219

P–K4; 15 B×Nch, P×B; 16 Q–K2 attacking the King Pawn and threatening B×P as well.

7	N–K2
8 B–Q3	QN–B3
9 Castles	Castles
10 Q–R5	N–N3

Parrying the mate threat. But White still maintains a strong attacking position.

11 R–B3	QN–K2
12 N–B3	P–QR3
13 QR–KB1	P–N4
14 N–Q1!	B–N2
15 N–B2	P–B5
16 N–N4!	. . . .

With this pretty idea: 16 . . . P×B; 17 N–B6ch!, P×N; 18 KP×P, N–B4; 19 R×N!, P×R; 20 Q–R6 forcing mate.

16	P–B4
17 P×P e.p.	N–B4
18 BP×P	N×NP

White has several winning lines now, but he finds the prettiest way.

Position after 18 . . . N×NP

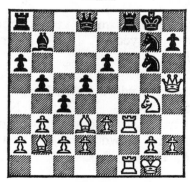

White now announced a beautiful forced mate:

19 Q×RPch!!	K×Q
20 R–R3ch	K–N1

The interpolation of 20 . . . Q–R5 lengthens the mating process by one move. On the other hand, if 20 . . . N–R4 there follows 21 R×Nch, K–N1; 22 R–R8ch!, N×R; 23 N–R6 mate.

21 N–R6ch	K–R1
22 N–B7 dbl ch	K–N1
23 R–R8ch!	N×R
24 N–R6 mate	

A most unusual finish. The whole key to White's successful attack lies in his far-sighted 7 P×B!

A CATALOG OF SELECTED DOVER
BOOKS IN ALL FIELDS OF INTEREST

CONCERNING THE SPIRITUAL IN ART, Wassily Kandinsky. Pioneering work by father of abstract art. Thoughts on color theory, nature of art. Analysis of earlier masters. 12 illustrations. 80pp. of text. 5⅜ × 8½.   23411-8 Pa. $3.95

ANIMALS: 1,419 Copyright-Free Illustrations of Mammals, Birds, Fish, Insects, etc., Jim Harter (ed.). Clear wood engravings present, in extremely lifelike poses, over 1,000 species of animals. One of the most extensive pictorial sourcebooks of its kind. Captions. Index. 284pp. 9 × 12.   23766-4 Pa. $12.95

CELTIC ART: The Methods of Construction, George Bain. Simple geometric techniques for making Celtic interlacements, spirals, Kells-type initials, animals, humans, etc. Over 500 illustrations. 160pp. 9 × 12. (USO)   22923-8 Pa. $9.95

AN ATLAS OF ANATOMY FOR ARTISTS, Fritz Schider. Most thorough reference work on art anatomy in the world. Hundreds of illustrations, including selections from works by Vesalius, Leonardo, Goya, Ingres, Michelangelo, others. 593 illustrations. 192pp. 7⅛ × 10¼.   20241-0 Pa. $9.95

CELTIC HAND STROKE-BY-STROKE (Irish Half-Uncial from "The Book of Kells"): An Arthur Baker Calligraphy Manual, Arthur Baker. Complete guide to creating each letter of the alphabet in distinctive Celtic manner. Covers hand position, strokes, pens, inks, paper, more. Illustrated. 48pp. 8¼ × 11.   24336-2 Pa. $3.95

EASY ORIGAMI, John Montroll. Charming collection of 32 projects (hat, cup, pelican, piano, swan, many more) specially designed for the novice origami hobbyist. Clearly illustrated easy-to-follow instructions insure that even beginning papercrafters will achieve successful results. 48pp. 8¼ × 11.   27298-2 Pa. $2.95

THE COMPLETE BOOK OF BIRDHOUSE CONSTRUCTION FOR WOOD-WORKERS, Scott D. Campbell. Detailed instructions, illustrations, tables. Also data on bird habitat and instinct patterns. Bibliography. 3 tables. 63 illustrations in 15 figures. 48pp. 5¼ × 8½.   24407-5 Pa. $1.95

BLOOMINGDALE'S ILLUSTRATED 1886 CATALOG: Fashions, Dry Goods and Housewares, Bloomingdale Brothers. Famed merchants' extremely rare catalog depicting about 1,700 products: clothing, housewares, firearms, dry goods, jewelry, more. Invaluable for dating, identifying vintage items. Also, copyright-free graphics for artists, designers. Co-published with Henry Ford Museum & Greenfield Village. 160pp. 8¼ × 11.   25780-0 Pa. $9.95

HISTORIC COSTUME IN PICTURES, Braun & Schneider. Over 1,450 costumed figures in clearly detailed engravings—from dawn of civilization to end of 19th century. Captions. Many folk costumes. 256pp. 8⅜ × 11¼.   23150-X Pa. $11.95

STICKLEY CRAFTSMAN FURNITURE CATALOGS, Gustav Stickley and L. & J. G. Stickley. Beautiful, functional furniture in two authentic catalogs from 1910. 594 illustrations, including 277 photos, show settles, rockers, armchairs, reclining chairs, bookcases, desks, tables. 183pp. 6½ × 9¼. 23838-5 Pa. **$9.95**

AMERICAN LOCOMOTIVES IN HISTORIC PHOTOGRAPHS: 1858 to 1949, Ron Ziel (ed.). A rare collection of 126 meticulously detailed official photographs, called "builder portraits," of American locomotives that majestically chronicle the rise of steam locomotive power in America. Introduction. Detailed captions. xi + 129pp. 9 × 12. 27393-8 Pa. **$12.95**

AMERICA'S LIGHTHOUSES: An Illustrated History, Francis Ross Holland, Jr. Delightfully written, profusely illustrated fact-filled survey of over 200 American lighthouses since 1716. History, anecdotes, technological advances, more. 240pp. 8 × 10¾. 25576-X Pa. **$11.95**

TOWARDS A NEW ARCHITECTURE, Le Corbusier. Pioneering manifesto by founder of "International School." Technical and aesthetic theories, views of industry, economics, relation of form to function, "mass-production split" and much more. Profusely illustrated. 320pp. 6⅛ × 9¼. (USO) 25023-7 Pa. **$9.95**

HOW THE OTHER HALF LIVES, Jacob Riis. Famous journalistic record, exposing poverty and degradation of New York slums around 1900, by major social reformer. 100 striking and influential photographs. 233pp. 10 × 7⅞. 22012-5 Pa **$10.95**

FRUIT KEY AND TWIG KEY TO TREES AND SHRUBS, William M. Harlow. One of the handiest and most widely used identification aids. Fruit key covers 120 deciduous and evergreen species; twig key 160 deciduous species. Easily used. Over 300 photographs. 126pp. 5⅜ × 8½. 20511-8 Pa. **$3.95**

COMMON BIRD SONGS, Dr. Donald J. Borror. Songs of 60 most common U.S. birds: robins, sparrows, cardinals, bluejays, finches, more—arranged in order of increasing complexity. Up to 9 variations of songs of each species.
Cassette and manual 99911-4 **$8.95**

ORCHIDS AS HOUSE PLANTS, Rebecca Tyson Northen. Grow cattleyas and many other kinds of orchids—in a window, in a case, or under artificial light. 63 illustrations. 148pp. 5⅜ × 8½. 23261-1 Pa. **$4.95**

MONSTER MAZES, Dave Phillips. Masterful mazes at four levels of difficulty. Avoid deadly perils and evil creatures to find magical treasures. Solutions for all 32 exciting illustrated puzzles. 48pp. 8¼ × 11. 26005-4 Pa. **$2.95**

MOZART'S DON GIOVANNI (DOVER OPERA LIBRETTO SERIES), Wolfgang Amadeus Mozart. Introduced and translated by Ellen H. Bleiler. Standard Italian libretto, with complete English translation. Convenient and thoroughly portable—an ideal companion for reading along with a recording or the performance itself. Introduction. List of characters. Plot summary. 121pp. 5¼ × 8½. 24944-1 Pa. **$2.95**

TECHNICAL MANUAL AND DICTIONARY OF CLASSICAL BALLET, Gail Grant. Defines, explains, comments on steps, movements, poses and concepts. 15-page pictorial section. Basic book for student, viewer. 127pp. 5⅜ × 8½. 21843-0 Pa. **$4.95**

BRASS INSTRUMENTS: Their History and Development, Anthony Baines. Authoritative, updated survey of the evolution of trumpets, trombones, bugles, cornets, French horns, tubas and other brass wind instruments. Over 140 illustrations and 48 music examples. Corrected and updated by author. New preface. Bibliography. 320pp. 5⅜ × 8½. 27574-4 Pa. $9.95

HOLLYWOOD GLAMOR PORTRAITS, John Kobal (ed.). 145 photos from 1926–49. Harlow, Gable, Bogart, Bacall; 94 stars in all. Full background on photographers, technical aspects. 160pp. 8⅜ × 11¼. 23352-9 Pa. $11.95

MAX AND MORITZ, Wilhelm Busch. Great humor classic in both German and English. Also 10 other works: "Cat and Mouse," "Plisch and Plumm," etc. 216pp. 5⅜ × 8½. 20181-3 Pa. $5.95

THE RAVEN AND OTHER FAVORITE POEMS, Edgar Allan Poe. Over 40 of the author's most memorable poems: "The Bells," "Ulalume," "Israfel," "To Helen," "The Conqueror Worm," "Eldorado," "Annabel Lee," many more. Alphabetic lists of titles and first lines. 64pp. 5³⁄₁₆ × 8¼. 26685-0 Pa. $1.00

SEVEN SCIENCE FICTION NOVELS, H. G. Wells. The standard collection of the great novels. Complete, unabridged. First Men in the Moon, Island of Dr. Moreau, War of the Worlds, Food of the Gods, Invisible Man, Time Machine, In the Days of the Comet. Total of 1,015pp. 5⅜ × 8½. (USO) 20264-X Clothbd. $29.95

AMULETS AND SUPERSTITIONS, E. A. Wallis Budge. Comprehensive discourse on origin, powers of amulets in many ancient cultures: Arab, Persian, Babylonian, Assyrian, Egyptian, Gnostic, Hebrew, Phoenician, Syriac, etc. Covers cross, swastika, crucifix, seals, rings, stones, etc. 584pp. 5⅜ × 8½. 23573-4 Pa. $12.95

RUSSIAN STORIES/PYCCKNE PACCKA3bl: A Dual-Language Book, edited by Gleb Struve. Twelve tales by such masters as Chekhov, Tolstoy, Dostoevsky, Pushkin, others. Excellent word-for-word English translations on facing pages, plus teaching and study aids, Russian/English vocabulary, biographical/critical introductions, more. 416pp. 5⅜ × 8½. 26244-8 Pa. $8.95

PHILADELPHIA THEN AND NOW: 60 Sites Photographed in the Past and Present, Kenneth Finkel and Susan Oyama. Rare photographs of City Hall, Logan Square, Independence Hall, Betsy Ross House, other landmarks juxtaposed with contemporary views. Captures changing face of historic city. Introduction. Captions. 128pp. 8¼ × 11. 25790-8 Pa. $9.95

AIA ARCHITECTURAL GUIDE TO NASSAU AND SUFFOLK COUNTIES, LONG ISLAND, The American Institute of Architects, Long Island Chapter, and the Society for the Preservation of Long Island Antiquities. Comprehensive, well-researched and generously illustrated volume brings to life over three centuries of Long Island's great architectural heritage. More than 240 photographs with authoritative, extensively detailed captions. 176pp. 8¼ × 11. 26946-9 Pa. $14.95

NORTH AMERICAN INDIAN LIFE: Customs and Traditions of 23 Tribes, Elsie Clews Parsons (ed.). 27 fictionalized essays by noted anthropologists examine religion, customs, government, additional facets of life among the Winnebago, Crow, Zuni, Eskimo, other tribes. 480pp. 6⅛ × 9¼. 27377-6 Pa. $10.95

FRANK LLOYD WRIGHT'S HOLLYHOCK HOUSE, Donald Hoffmann. Lavishly illustrated, carefully documented study of one of Wright's most controversial residential designs. Over 120 photographs, floor plans, elevations, etc. Detailed perceptive text by noted Wright scholar. Index. 128pp. 9¼ × 10¾.
27133-1 Pa. $11.95

THE MALE AND FEMALE FIGURE IN MOTION: 60 Classic Photographic Sequences, Eadweard Muybridge. 60 true-action photographs of men and women walking, running, climbing, bending, turning, etc., reproduced from rare 19th-century masterpiece. vi + 121pp. 9 × 12. 24745-7 Pa. $10.95

1001 QUESTIONS ANSWERED ABOUT THE SEASHORE, N. J. Berrill and Jacquelyn Berrill. Queries answered about dolphins, sea snails, sponges, starfish, fishes, shore birds, many others. Covers appearance, breeding, growth, feeding, much more. 305pp. 5¼ × 8¼. 23366-9 Pa. $7.95

GUIDE TO OWL WATCHING IN NORTH AMERICA, Donald S. Heintzelman. Superb guide offers complete data and descriptions of 19 species: barn owl, screech owl, snowy owl, many more. Expert coverage of owl-watching equipment, conservation, migrations and invasions, etc. Guide to observing sites. 84 illustrations. xiii + 193pp. 5⅜ × 8½. 27344-X Pa. $8.95

MEDICINAL AND OTHER USES OF NORTH AMERICAN PLANTS: A Historical Survey with Special Reference to the Eastern Indian Tribes, Charlotte Erichsen-Brown. Chronological historical citations document 500 years of usage of plants, trees, shrubs native to eastern Canada, northeastern U.S. Also complete identifying information. 343 illustrations. 544pp. 6½ × 9¼. 25951-X Pa. $12.95

STORYBOOK MAZES, Dave Phillips. 23 stories and mazes on two-page spreads: Wizard of Oz, Treasure Island, Robin Hood, etc. Solutions. 64pp. 8¼ × 11.
23628-5 Pa. $2.95

NEGRO FOLK MUSIC, U.S.A., Harold Courlander. Noted folklorist's scholarly yet readable analysis of rich and varied musical tradition. Includes authentic versions of over 40 folk songs. Valuable bibliography and discography. xi + 324pp. 5⅜ × 8½. 27350-4 Pa. $7.95

MOVIE-STAR PORTRAITS OF THE FORTIES, John Kobal (ed.). 163 glamor, studio photos of 106 stars of the 1940s: Rita Hayworth, Ava Gardner, Marlon Brando, Clark Gable, many more. 176pp. 8⅜ × 11¼. 23546-7 Pa. $11.95

BENCHLEY LOST AND FOUND, Robert Benchley. Finest humor from early 30s, about pet peeves, child psychologists, post office and others. Mostly unavailable elsewhere. 73 illustrations by Peter Arno and others. 183pp. 5⅜ × 8½.
22410-4 Pa. $5.95

YEKL and THE IMPORTED BRIDEGROOM AND OTHER STORIES OF YIDDISH NEW YORK, Abraham Cahan. Film Hester Street based on Yekl (1896). Novel, other stories among first about Jewish immigrants on N.Y.'s East Side. 240pp. 5⅜ × 8½. 22427-9 Pa. $6.95

SELECTED POEMS, Walt Whitman. Generous sampling from *Leaves of Grass*. Twenty-four poems include "I Hear America Singing," "Song of the Open Road," "I Sing the Body Electric," "When Lilacs Last in the Dooryard Bloom'd," "O Captain! My Captain!"—all reprinted from an authoritative edition. Lists of titles and first lines. 128pp. 5³⁄₁₆ × 8¼. 26878-0 Pa. $1.00

THE BEST TALES OF HOFFMANN, E. T. A. Hoffmann. 10 of Hoffmann's most important stories: "Nutcracker and the King of Mice," "The Golden Flowerpot," etc. 458pp. 5⅜ × 8½. 21793-0 Pa. $8.95

FROM FETISH TO GOD IN ANCIENT EGYPT, E. A. Wallis Budge. Rich detailed survey of Egyptian conception of "God" and gods, magic, cult of animals, Osiris, more. Also, superb English translations of hymns and legends. 240 illustrations. 545pp. 5⅜ × 8½. 25803-3 Pa. $11.95

FRENCH STORIES/CONTES FRANÇAIS: A Dual-Language Book, Wallace Fowlie. Ten stories by French masters, Voltaire to Camus: "Micromegas" by Voltaire; "The Atheist's Mass" by Balzac; "Minuet" by de Maupassant; "The Guest" by Camus, six more. Excellent English translations on facing pages. Also French-English vocabulary list, exercises, more. 352pp. 5⅜ × 8½. 26443-2 Pa. $8.95

CHICAGO AT THE TURN OF THE CENTURY IN PHOTOGRAPHS: 122 Historic Views from the Collections of the Chicago Historical Society, Larry A. Viskochil. Rare large-format prints offer detailed views of City Hall, State Street, the Loop, Hull House, Union Station, many other landmarks, circa 1904–1913. Introduction. Captions. Maps. 144pp. 9⅜ × 12¼. 24656-6 Pa. $12.95

OLD BROOKLYN IN EARLY PHOTOGRAPHS, 1865–1929, William Lee Younger. Luna Park, Gravesend race track, construction of Grand Army Plaza, moving of Hotel Brighton, etc. 157 previously unpublished photographs. 165pp. 8⅞ × 11¾. 23587-4 Pa. $13.95

THE MYTHS OF THE NORTH AMERICAN INDIANS, Lewis Spence. Rich anthology of the myths and legends of the Algonquins, Iroquois, Pawnees and Sioux, prefaced by an extensive historical and ethnological commentary. 36 illustrations. 480pp. 5⅜ × 8½. 25967-6 Pa. $8.95

AN ENCYCLOPEDIA OF BATTLES: Accounts of Over 1,560 Battles from 1479 B.C. to the Present, David Eggenberger. Essential details of every major battle in recorded history from the first battle of Megiddo in 1479 B.C. to Grenada in 1984. List of Battle Maps. New Appendix covering the years 1967–1984. Index. 99 illustrations. 544pp. 6½ × 9¼. 24913-1 Pa. $14.95

SAILING ALONE AROUND THE WORLD, Captain Joshua Slocum. First man to sail around the world, alone, in small boat. One of great feats of seamanship told in delightful manner. 67 illustrations. 294pp. 5⅜ × 8½. 20326-3 Pa. $5.95

ANARCHISM AND OTHER ESSAYS, Emma Goldman. Powerful, penetrating, prophetic essays on direct action, role of minorities, prison reform, puritan hypocrisy, violence, etc. 271pp. 5⅜ × 8½. 22484-8 Pa. $5.95

MYTHS OF THE HINDUS AND BUDDHISTS, Ananda K. Coomaraswamy and Sister Nivedita. Great stories of the epics; deeds of Krishna, Shiva, taken from puranas, Vedas, folk tales; etc. 32 illustrations. 400pp. 5⅜ × 8½. 21759-0 Pa. $9.95

BEYOND PSYCHOLOGY, Otto Rank. Fear of death, desire of immortality, nature of sexuality, social organization, creativity, according to Rankian system. 291pp. 5⅜ × 8½. 20485-5 Pa. $8.95

A THEOLOGICO-POLITICAL TREATISE, Benedict Spinoza. Also contains unfinished Political Treatise. Great classic on religious liberty, theory of government on common consent. R. Elwes translation. Total of 421pp. 5⅜ × 8½. 20249-6 Pa. $8.95

MY BONDAGE AND MY FREEDOM, Frederick Douglass. Born a slave, Douglass became outspoken force in antislavery movement. The best of Douglass' autobiographies. Graphic description of slave life. 464pp. 5⅜ × 8½.　22457-0 Pa. $8.95

FOLLOWING THE EQUATOR: A Journey Around the World, Mark Twain. Fascinating humorous account of 1897 voyage to Hawaii, Australia, India, New Zealand, etc. Ironic, bemused reports on peoples, customs, climate, flora and fauna, politics, much more. 197 illustrations. 720pp. 5⅜ × 8½.　26113-1 Pa. $15.95

THE PEOPLE CALLED SHAKERS, Edward D. Andrews. Definitive study of Shakers: origins, beliefs, practices, dances, social organization, furniture and crafts, etc. 33 illustrations. 351pp. 5⅜ × 8½.　21081-2 Pa. $8.95

THE MYTHS OF GREECE AND ROME, H. A. Guerber. A classic of mythology, generously illustrated, long prized for its simple, graphic, accurate retelling of the principal myths of Greece and Rome, and for its commentary on their origins and significance. With 64 illustrations by Michelangelo, Raphael, Titian, Rubens, Canova, Bernini and others. 480pp. 5⅜ × 8½.　27584-1 Pa. $9.95

PSYCHOLOGY OF MUSIC, Carl E. Seashore. Classic work discusses music as a medium from psychological viewpoint. Clear treatment of physical acoustics, auditory apparatus, sound perception, development of musical skills, nature of musical feeling, host of other topics. 88 figures. 408pp. 5⅜ × 8½. 21851-1 Pa. $9.95

THE PHILOSOPHY OF HISTORY, Georg W. Hegel. Great classic of Western thought develops concept that history is not chance but rational process, the evolution of freedom. 457pp. 5⅜ × 8½.　20112-0 Pa. $9.95

THE BOOK OF TEA, Kakuzo Okakura. Minor classic of the Orient: entertaining, charming explanation, interpretation of traditional Japanese culture in terms of tea ceremony. 94pp. 5⅜ × 8½.　20070-1 Pa. $3.95

LIFE IN ANCIENT EGYPT, Adolf Erman. Fullest, most thorough, detailed older account with much not in more recent books, domestic life, religion, magic, medicine, commerce, much more. Many illustrations reproduce tomb paintings, carvings, hieroglyphs, etc. 597pp. 5⅜ × 8½.　22632-8 Pa. $10.95

SUNDIALS, Their Theory and Construction, Albert Waugh. Far and away the best, most thorough coverage of ideas, mathematics concerned, types, construction, adjusting anywhere. Simple, nontechnical treatment allows even children to build several of these dials. Over 100 illustrations. 230pp. 5⅜ × 8½.　22947-5 Pa. $7.95

DYNAMICS OF FLUIDS IN POROUS MEDIA, Jacob Bear. For advanced students of ground water hydrology, soil mechanics and physics, drainage and irrigation engineering, and more. 335 illustrations. Exercises, with answers. 784pp. 6⅛ × 9¼.　65675-6 Pa. $19.95

SONGS OF EXPERIENCE: Facsimile Reproduction with 26 Plates in Full Color, William Blake. 26 full-color plates from a rare 1826 edition. Includes "The Tyger," "London," "Holy Thursday," and other poems. Printed text of poems. 48pp. 5¼ × 7.　24636-1 Pa. $4.95

OLD-TIME VIGNETTES IN FULL COLOR, Carol Belanger Grafton (ed.). Over 390 charming, often sentimental illustrations, selected from archives of Victorian graphics—pretty women posing, children playing, food, flowers, kittens and puppies, smiling cherubs, birds and butterflies, much more. All copyright-free. 48pp. 9¼ × 12¼.　27269-9 Pa. $5.95

PERSPECTIVE FOR ARTISTS, Rex Vicat Cole. Depth, perspective of sky and sea, shadows, much more, not usually covered. 391 diagrams, 81 reproductions of drawings and paintings. 279pp. 5⅜ × 8½. 22487-2 Pa. $6.95

DRAWING THE LIVING FIGURE, Joseph Sheppard. Innovative approach to artistic anatomy focuses on specifics of surface anatomy, rather than muscles and bones. Over 170 drawings of live models in front, back and side views, and in widely varying poses. Accompanying diagrams. 177 illustrations. Introduction. Index. 144pp. 8⅜ × 11¼. 26723-7 Pa. $8.95

GOTHIC AND OLD ENGLISH ALPHABETS: 100 Complete Fonts, Dan X. Solo. Add power, elegance to posters, signs, other graphics with 100 stunning copyright-free alphabets: Blackstone, Dolbey, Germania, 97 more—including many lower-case, numerals, punctuation marks. 104pp. 8⅛ × 11. 24695-7 Pa. $8.95

HOW TO DO BEADWORK, Mary White. Fundamental book on craft from simple projects to five-bead chains and woven works. 106 illustrations. 142pp. 5⅜ × 8. 20697-1 Pa. $4.95

THE BOOK OF WOOD CARVING, Charles Marshall Sayers. Finest book for beginners discusses fundamentals and offers 34 designs. "Absolutely first rate . . . well thought out and well executed."—E. J. Tangerman. 118pp. 7¾ × 10⅝. 23654-4 Pa. $5.95

ILLUSTRATED CATALOG OF CIVIL WAR MILITARY GOODS: Union Army Weapons, Insignia, Uniform Accessories, and Other Equipment, Schuyler, Hartley, and Graham. Rare, profusely illustrated 1846 catalog includes Union Army uniform and dress regulations, arms and ammunition, coats, insignia, flags, swords, rifles, etc. 226 illustrations. 160pp. 9 × 12. 24939-5 Pa. $10.95

WOMEN'S FASHIONS OF THE EARLY 1900s: An Unabridged Republication of "New York Fashions, 1909," National Cloak & Suit Co. Rare catalog of mail-order fashions documents women's and children's clothing styles shortly after the turn of the century. Captions offer full descriptions, prices. Invaluable resource for fashion, costume historians. Approximately 725 illustrations. 128pp. 8⅜ × 11¼. 27276-1 Pa. $11.95

THE 1912 AND 1915 GUSTAV STICKLEY FURNITURE CATALOGS, Gustav Stickley. With over 200 detailed illustrations and descriptions, these two catalogs are essential reading and reference materials and identification guides for Stickley furniture. Captions cite materials, dimensions and prices. 112pp. 6½ × 9¼. 26676-1 Pa. $9.95

EARLY AMERICAN LOCOMOTIVES, John H. White, Jr. Finest locomotive engravings from early 19th century: historical (1804–74), main-line (after 1870), special, foreign, etc. 147 plates. 142pp. 11⅜ × 8¼. 22772-3 Pa. $10.95

THE TALL SHIPS OF TODAY IN PHOTOGRAPHS, Frank O. Braynard. Lavishly illustrated tribute to nearly 100 majestic contemporary sailing vessels: Amerigo Vespucci, Clearwater, Constitution, Eagle, Mayflower, Sea Cloud, Victory, many more. Authoritative captions provide statistics, background on each ship. 190 black-and-white photographs and illustrations. Introduction. 128pp. 8⅞ × 11¾. 27163-3 Pa. $13.95

CATALOG OF DOVER BOOKS

EARLY NINETEENTH-CENTURY CRAFTS AND TRADES, Peter Stockham (ed.). Extremely rare 1807 volume describes to youngsters the crafts and trades of the day: brickmaker, weaver, dressmaker, bookbinder, ropemaker, saddler, many more. Quaint prose, charming illustrations for each craft. 20 black-and-white line illustrations. 192pp. 4⅜ × 6. 27293-1 Pa. $4.95

VICTORIAN FASHIONS AND COSTUMES FROM HARPER'S BAZAR, 1867–1898, Stella Blum (ed.). Day costumes, evening wear, sports clothes, shoes, hats, other accessories in over 1,000 detailed engravings. 320pp. 9⅜ × 12¼.
22990-4 Pa. $13.95

GUSTAV STICKLEY, THE CRAFTSMAN, Mary Ann Smith. Superb study surveys broad scope of Stickley's achievement, especially in architecture. Design philosophy, rise and fall of the Craftsman empire, descriptions and floor plans for many Craftsman houses, more. 86 black-and-white halftones. 31 line illustrations. Introduction. 208pp. 6½ × 9¼. 27210-9 Pa. $9.95

THE LONG ISLAND RAIL ROAD IN EARLY PHOTOGRAPHS, Ron Ziel. Over 220 rare photos, informative text document origin (1844) and development of rail service on Long Island. Vintage views of early trains, locomotives, stations, passengers, crews, much more. Captions. 8⅞ × 11¾. 26301-0 Pa. $13.95

THE BOOK OF OLD SHIPS: From Egyptian Galleys to Clipper Ships, Henry B. Culver. Superb, authoritative history of sailing vessels, with 80 magnificent line illustrations. Galley, bark, caravel, longship, whaler, many more. Detailed, informative text on each vessel by noted naval historian. Introduction. 256pp. 5⅜ × 8½. 27332-6 Pa. $6.95

TEN BOOKS ON ARCHITECTURE, Vitruvius. The most important book ever written on architecture. Early Roman aesthetics, technology, classical orders, site selection, all other aspects. Morgan translation. 331pp. 5⅜ × 8½. 20645-9 Pa. $8.95

THE HUMAN FIGURE IN MOTION, Eadweard Muybridge. More than 4,500 stopped-action photos, in action series, showing undraped men, women, children jumping, lying down, throwing, sitting, wrestling, carrying, etc. 390pp. 7⅞ × 10⅝.
20204-6 Clothbd. $24.95

TREES OF THE EASTERN AND CENTRAL UNITED STATES AND CANADA, William M. Harlow. Best one-volume guide to 140 trees. Full descriptions, woodlore, range, etc. Over 600 illustrations. Handy size. 288pp. 4½ × 6⅜.
20395-6 Pa. $5.95

SONGS OF WESTERN BIRDS, Dr. Donald J. Borror. Complete song and call repertoire of 60 western species, including flycatchers, juncoes, cactus wrens, many more—includes fully illustrated booklet. Cassette and manual 99913-0 $8.95

GROWING AND USING HERBS AND SPICES, Milo Miloradovich. Versatile handbook provides all the information needed for cultivation and use of all the herbs and spices available in North America. 4 illustrations. Index. Glossary. 236pp. 5⅜ × 8½. 25058-X Pa. $6.95

BIG BOOK OF MAZES AND LABYRINTHS, Walter Shepherd. 50 mazes and labyrinths in all—classical, solid, ripple, and more—in one great volume. Perfect inexpensive puzzler for clever youngsters. Full solutions. 112pp. 8⅛ × 11.
22951-3 Pa. $4.95

PIANO TUNING, J. Cree Fischer. Clearest, best book for beginner, amateur. Simple repairs, raising dropped notes, tuning by easy method of flattened fifths. No previous skills needed. 4 illustrations. 201pp. 5⅜ × 8½.   23267-0 Pa. $5.95

A SOURCE BOOK IN THEATRICAL HISTORY, A. M. Nagler. Contemporary observers on acting, directing, make-up, costuming, stage props, machinery, scene design, from Ancient Greece to Chekhov. 611pp. 5⅜ × 8½.   20515-0 Pa. $11.95

THE COMPLETE NONSENSE OF EDWARD LEAR, Edward Lear. All nonsense limericks, zany alphabets, Owl and Pussycat, songs, nonsense botany, etc., illustrated by Lear. Total of 320pp. 5⅜ × 8½. (USO)   20167-8 Pa. $6.95

VICTORIAN PARLOUR POETRY: An Annotated Anthology, Michael R. Turner. 117 gems by Longfellow, Tennyson, Browning, many lesser-known poets. "The Village Blacksmith," "Curfew Must Not Ring Tonight," "Only a Baby Small," dozens more, often difficult to find elsewhere. Index of poets, titles, first lines. xxiii + 325pp. 5⅜ × 8¼.   27044-0 Pa. $8.95

DUBLINERS, James Joyce. Fifteen stories offer vivid, tightly focused observations of the lives of Dublin's poorer classes. At least one, "The Dead," is considered a masterpiece. Reprinted complete and unabridged from standard edition. 160pp. 5³⁄₁₆ × 8¼.   26870-5 Pa. $1.00

THE HAUNTED MONASTERY and THE CHINESE MAZE MURDERS, Robert van Gulik. Two full novels by van Gulik, set in 7th-century China, continue adventures of Judge Dee and his companions. An evil Taoist monastery, seemingly supernatural events; overgrown topiary maze hides strange crimes. 27 illustrations. 328pp. 5⅜ × 8½.   23502-5 Pa. $7.95

THE BOOK OF THE SACRED MAGIC OF ABRAMELIN THE MAGE, translated by S. MacGregor Mathers. Medieval manuscript of ceremonial magic. Basic document in Aleister Crowley, Golden Dawn groups. 268pp. 5⅜ × 8½.
                    23211-5 Pa. $8.95

NEW RUSSIAN-ENGLISH AND ENGLISH-RUSSIAN DICTIONARY, M. A. O'Brien. This is a remarkably handy Russian dictionary, containing a surprising amount of information, including over 70,000 entries. 366pp. 4½ × 6⅛.
                    20208-9 Pa. $9.95

HISTORIC HOMES OF THE AMERICAN PRESIDENTS, Second, Revised Edition, Irvin Haas. A traveler's guide to American Presidential homes, most open to the public, depicting and describing homes occupied by every American President from George Washington to George Bush. With visiting hours, admission charges, travel routes. 175 photographs. Index. 160pp. 8¼ × 11. 26751-2 Pa. $10.95

NEW YORK IN THE FORTIES, Andreas Feininger. 162 brilliant photographs by the well-known photographer, formerly with *Life* magazine. Commuters, shoppers, Times Square at night, much else from city at its peak. Captions by John von Hartz. 181pp. 9¼ × 10¾.   23585-8 Pa. $12.95

INDIAN SIGN LANGUAGE, William Tomkins. Over 525 signs developed by Sioux and other tribes. Written instructions and diagrams. Also 290 pictographs. 111pp. 6⅛ × 9¼.   22029-X Pa. $3.50

ANATOMY: A Complete Guide for Artists, Joseph Sheppard. A master of figure drawing shows artists how to render human anatomy convincingly. Over 460 illustrations. 224pp. 8⅜ × 11¼. 27279-6 Pa. $10.95

MEDIEVAL CALLIGRAPHY: Its History and Technique, Marc Drogin. Spirited history, comprehensive instruction manual covers 13 styles (ca. 4th century thru 15th). Excellent photographs; directions for duplicating medieval techniques with modern tools. 224pp. 8⅜ × 11¼. 26142-5 Pa. $11.95

DRIED FLOWERS: How to Prepare Them, Sarah Whitlock and Martha Rankin. Complete instructions on how to use silica gel, meal and borax, perlite aggregate, sand and borax, glycerine and water to create attractive permanent flower arrangements. 12 illustrations. 32pp. 5⅜ × 8½. 21802-3 Pa. $1.00

EASY-TO-MAKE BIRD FEEDERS FOR WOODWORKERS, Scott D. Campbell. Detailed, simple-to-use guide for designing, constructing, caring for and using feeders. Text, illustrations for 12 classic and contemporary designs. 96pp. 5⅜ × 8½. 25847-5 Pa. $2.95

OLD-TIME CRAFTS AND TRADES, Peter Stockham. An 1807 book created to teach children about crafts and trades open to them as future careers. It describes in detailed, nontechnical terms 24 different occupations, among them coachmaker, gardener, hairdresser, lacemaker, shoemaker, wheelwright, copper-plate printer, milliner, trunkmaker, merchant and brewer. Finely detailed engravings illustrate each occupation. 192pp. 4⅝ × 6. 27398-9 Pa. $4.95

THE HISTORY OF UNDERCLOTHES, C. Willett Cunnington and Phyllis Cunnington. Fascinating, well-documented survey covering six centuries of English undergarments, enhanced with over 100 illustrations: 12th-century laced-up bodice, footed long drawers (1795), 19th-century bustles, 19th-century corsets for men, Victorian "bust improvers," much more. 272pp. 5⅜ × 8¼. 27124-2 Pa. $9.95

ARTS AND CRAFTS FURNITURE: The Complete Brooks Catalog of 1912, Brooks Manufacturing Co. Photos and detailed descriptions of more than 150 now very collectible furniture designs from the Arts and Crafts movement depict davenports, settees, buffets, desks, tables, chairs, bedsteads, dressers and more, all built of solid, quarter-sawed oak. Invaluable for students and enthusiasts of antiques, Americana and the decorative arts. 80pp. 6½ × 9¼. 27471-3 Pa. $7.95

HOW WE INVENTED THE AIRPLANE: An Illustrated History, Orville Wright. Fascinating firsthand account covers early experiments, construction of planes and motors, first flights, much more. Introduction and commentary by Fred C. Kelly. 76 photographs. 96pp. 8¼ × 11. 25662-6 Pa. $8.95

THE ARTS OF THE SAILOR: Knotting, Splicing and Ropework, Hervey Garrett Smith. Indispensable shipboard reference covers tools, basic knots and useful hitches; handsewing and canvas work, more. Over 100 illustrations. Delightful reading for sea lovers. 256pp. 5⅜ × 8½. 26440-8 Pa. $7.95

FRANK LLOYD WRIGHT'S FALLINGWATER: The House and Its History, Second, Revised Edition, Donald Hoffmann. A total revision—both in text and illustrations—of the standard document on Fallingwater, the boldest, most personal architectural statement of Wright's mature years, updated with valuable new material from the recently opened Frank Lloyd Wright Archives. "Fascinating"—*The New York Times.* 116 illustrations. 128pp. 9¼ × 10¾. 27430-6 Pa. $10.95

PHOTOGRAPHIC SKETCHBOOK OF THE CIVIL WAR, Alexander Gardner. 100 photos taken on field during the Civil War. Famous shots of Manassas, Harper's Ferry, Lincoln, Richmond, slave pens, etc. 244pp. 10⅝ × 8¼.
22731-6 Pa. $9.95

FIVE ACRES AND INDEPENDENCE, Maurice G. Kains. Great back-to-the-land classic explains basics of self-sufficient farming. The one book to get. 95 illustrations. 397pp. 5⅜ × 8½. 20974-1 Pa. $7.95

SONGS OF EASTERN BIRDS, Dr. Donald J. Borror. Songs and calls of 60 species most common to eastern U.S.: warblers, woodpeckers, flycatchers, thrushes, larks, many more in high-quality recording. Cassette and manual 99912-2 $8.95

A MODERN HERBAL, Margaret Grieve. Much the fullest, most exact, most useful compilation of herbal material. Gigantic alphabetical encyclopedia, from aconite to zedoary, gives botanical information, medical properties, folklore, economic uses, much else. Indispensable to serious reader. 161 illustrations. 888pp. 6½ × 9¼. 2-vol. set. (USO) Vol. I: 22798-7 Pa. $9.95
Vol. II: 22799-5 Pa. $9.95

HIDDEN TREASURE MAZE BOOK, Dave Phillips. Solve 34 challenging mazes accompanied by heroic tales of adventure. Evil dragons, people-eating plants, bloodthirsty giants, many more dangerous adversaries lurk at every twist and turn. 34 mazes, stories, solutions. 48pp. 8¼ × 11. 24566-7 Pa. $2.95

LETTERS OF W. A. MOZART, Wolfgang A. Mozart. Remarkable letters show bawdy wit, humor, imagination, musical insights, contemporary musical world; includes some letters from Leopold Mozart. 276pp. 5⅜ × 8½. 22859-2 Pa. $7.95

BASIC PRINCIPLES OF CLASSICAL BALLET, Agrippina Vaganova. Great Russian theoretician, teacher explains methods for teaching classical ballet. 118 illustrations. 175pp. 5⅜ × 8½. 22036-2 Pa. $4.95

THE JUMPING FROG, Mark Twain. Revenge edition. The original story of The Celebrated Jumping Frog of Calaveras County, a hapless French translation, and Twain's hilarious "retranslation" from the French. 12 illustrations. 66pp. 5⅜ × 8½.
22686-7 Pa. $3.95

BEST REMEMBERED POEMS, Martin Gardner (ed.). The 126 poems in this superb collection of 19th- and 20th-century British and American verse range from Shelley's "To a Skylark" to the impassioned "Renascence" of Edna St. Vincent Millay and to Edward Lear's whimsical "The Owl and the Pussycat." 224pp. 5⅜ × 8½.
27165-X Pa. $4.95

COMPLETE SONNETS, William Shakespeare. Over 150 exquisite poems deal with love, friendship, the tyranny of time, beauty's evanescence, death and other themes in language of remarkable power, precision and beauty. Glossary of archaic terms. 80pp. 5³⁄₁₆ × 8¼. 26686-9 Pa. $1.00

BODIES IN A BOOKSHOP, R. T. Campbell. Challenging mystery of blackmail and murder with ingenious plot and superbly drawn characters. In the best tradition of British suspense fiction. 192pp. 5⅜ × 8½. 24720-1 Pa. $5.95

THE WIT AND HUMOR OF OSCAR WILDE, Alvin Redman (ed.). More than 1,000 ripostes, paradoxes, wisecracks: Work is the curse of the drinking classes; I can resist everything except temptation; etc. 258pp. 5⅜ × 8½. **20602-5 Pa. $5.95**

SHAKESPEARE LEXICON AND QUOTATION DICTIONARY, Alexander Schmidt. Full definitions, locations, shades of meaning in every word in plays and poems. More than 50,000 exact quotations. 1,485pp. 6½ × 9¼. 2-vol. set.
Vol. I: **22726-X Pa. $16.95**
Vol. 2: 22727-8 Pa. $15.95

SELECTED POEMS, Emily Dickinson. Over 100 best-known, best-loved poems by one of America's foremost poets, reprinted from authoritative early editions. No comparable edition at this price. Index of first lines. 64pp. 5³⁄₁₆ × 8¼.
26466-1 Pa. $1.00

CELEBRATED CASES OF JUDGE DEE (DEE GOONG AN), translated by Robert van Gulik. Authentic 18th-century Chinese detective novel; Dee and associates solve three interlocked cases. Led to van Gulik's own stories with same characters. Extensive introduction. 9 illustrations. 237pp. 5⅜ × 8½.
23337-5 Pa. $6.95

THE MALLEUS MALEFICARUM OF KRAMER AND SPRENGER, translated by Montague Summers. Full text of most important witchhunter's "bible," used by both Catholics and Protestants. 278pp. 6⅝ × 10. **22802-9 Pa. $11.95**

SPANISH STORIES/CUENTOS ESPAÑOLES: A Dual-Language Book, Angel Flores (ed.). Unique format offers 13 great stories in Spanish by Cervantes, Borges, others. Faithful English translations on facing pages. 352pp. 5⅜ × 8½.
25399-6 Pa. $8.95

THE CHICAGO WORLD'S FAIR OF 1893: A Photographic Record, Stanley Appelbaum (ed.). 128 rare photos show 200 buildings, Beaux-Arts architecture, Midway, original Ferris Wheel, Edison's kinetoscope, more. Architectural emphasis; full text. 116pp. 8¼ × 11. 23990-X Pa. $9.95

OLD QUEENS, N.Y., IN EARLY PHOTOGRAPHS, Vincent F. Seyfried and William Asadorian. Over 160 rare photographs of Maspeth, Jamaica, Jackson Heights, and other areas. Vintage views of DeWitt Clinton mansion, 1939 World's Fair and more. Captions. 192pp. 8⅞ × 11. 26358-4 Pa. $12.95

CAPTURED BY THE INDIANS: 15 Firsthand Accounts, 1750–1870, Frederick Drimmer. Astounding true historical accounts of grisly torture, bloody conflicts, relentless pursuits, miraculous escapes and more, by people who lived to tell the tale. 384pp. 5⅜ × 8½. **24901-8 Pa. $8.95**

THE WORLD'S GREAT SPEECHES, Lewis Copeland and Lawrence W. Lamm (eds.). Vast collection of 278 speeches of Greeks to 1970. Powerful and effective models; unique look at history. 842pp. 5⅜ × 8½. **20468-5 Pa. $14.95**

THE BOOK OF THE SWORD, Sir Richard F. Burton. Great Victorian scholar/adventurer's eloquent, erudite history of the "queen of weapons"—from prehistory to early Roman Empire. Evolution and development of early swords, variations (sabre, broadsword, cutlass, scimitar, etc.), much more. 336pp. 6⅛ × 9¼. 25434-8 Pa. $8.95

AUTOBIOGRAPHY: The Story of My Experiments with Truth, Mohandas K. Gandhi. Boyhood, legal studies, purification, the growth of the Satyagraha (nonviolent protest) movement. Critical, inspiring work of the man responsible for the freedom of India. 480pp. 5⅜ × 8½. (USO) 24593-4 Pa. **$8.95**

CELTIC MYTHS AND LEGENDS, T. W. Rolleston. Masterful retelling of Irish and Welsh stories and tales. Cuchulain, King Arthur, Deirdre, the Grail, many more. First paperback edition. 58 full-page illustrations. 512pp. 5⅜ × 8½. 26507-2 Pa. $9.95

THE PRINCIPLES OF PSYCHOLOGY, William James. Famous long course complete, unabridged. Stream of thought, time perception, memory, experimental methods; great work decades ahead of its time. 94 figures. 1,391pp. 5⅜ × 8½. 2-vol. set.
Vol. I: 20381-6 Pa. $12.95
Vol. II: 20382-4 Pa. $12.95

THE WORLD AS WILL AND REPRESENTATION, Arthur Schopenhauer. Definitive English translation of Schopenhauer's life work, correcting more than 1,000 errors, omissions in earlier translations. Translated by E. F. J. Payne. Total of 1,269pp. 5⅜ × 8½. 2-vol. set.
Vol. 1: 21761-2 Pa. $11.95
Vol. 2: 21762-0 Pa. $11.95

MAGIC AND MYSTERY IN TIBET, Madame Alexandra David-Neel. Experiences among lamas, magicians, sages, sorcerers, Bonpa wizards. A true psychic discovery. 32 illustrations. 321pp. 5⅜ × 8½. (USO) 22682-4 Pa. $8.95

THE EGYPTIAN BOOK OF THE DEAD, E. A. Wallis Budge. Complete reproduction of Ani's papyrus, finest ever found. Full hieroglyphic text, interlinear transliteration, word-for-word translation, smooth translation. 533pp. 6½ × 9¼. 21866-X Pa. $9.95

MATHEMATICS FOR THE NONMATHEMATICIAN, Morris Kline. Detailed, college-level treatment of mathematics in cultural and historical context, with numerous exercises. Recommended Reading Lists. Tables. Numerous figures. 641pp. 5⅜ × 8½. 24823-2 Pa. $11.95

THEORY OF WING SECTIONS: Including a Summary of Airfoil Data, Ira H. Abbott and A. E. von Doenhoff. Concise compilation of subsonic aerodynamic characteristics of NACA wing sections, plus description of theory. 350pp. of tables. 693pp. 5⅜ × 8½. 60586-8 Pa. $14.95

THE RIME OF THE ANCIENT MARINER, Gustave Doré, S. T. Coleridge. Doré's finest work; 34 plates capture moods, subtleties of poem. Flawless full-size reproductions printed on facing pages with authoritative text of poem. "Beautiful. Simply beautiful."—*Publisher's Weekly*. 77pp. 9¼ × 12. 22305-1 Pa. $6.95

NORTH AMERICAN INDIAN DESIGNS FOR ARTISTS AND CRAFTSPEOPLE, Eva Wilson. Over 360 authentic copyright-free designs adapted from Navajo blankets, Hopi pottery, Sioux buffalo hides, more. Geometrics, symbolic figures, plant and animal motifs, etc. 128pp. 8⅜ × 11. (EUK) 25341-4 Pa. $7.95

SCULPTURE: Principles and Practice, Louis Slobodkin. Step-by-step approach to clay, plaster, metals, stone; classical and modern. 253 drawings, photos. 255pp. 8⅛ × 11. 22960-2 Pa. $10.95

CATALOG OF DOVER BOOKS

THE INFLUENCE OF SEA POWER UPON HISTORY, 1660–1783, A. T. Mahan. Influential classic of naval history and tactics still used as text in war colleges. First paperback edition. 4 maps. 24 battle plans. 640pp. 5⅜ × 8½.
25509-3 Pa. $12.95

THE STORY OF THE TITANIC AS TOLD BY ITS SURVIVORS, Jack Winocour (ed.). What it was really like. Panic, despair, shocking inefficiency, and a little heroism. More thrilling than any fictional account. 26 illustrations. 320pp. 5⅜ × 8½.
20610-6 Pa. $8.95

FAIRY AND FOLK TALES OF THE IRISH PEASANTRY, William Butler Yeats (ed.). Treasury of 64 tales from the twilight world of Celtic myth and legend: "The Soul Cages," "The Kildare Pooka," "King O'Toole and his Goose," many more. Introduction and Notes by W. B. Yeats. 352pp. 5⅜ × 8½. 26941-8 Pa. $8.95

BUDDHIST MAHAYANA TEXTS, E. B. Cowell and Others (eds.). Superb, accurate translations of basic documents in Mahayana Buddhism, highly important in history of religions. The Buddha-karita of Asvaghosha, Larger Sukhavativyuha, more. 448pp. 5⅜ × 8½. 25552-2 Pa. $9.95

ONE TWO THREE . . . INFINITY: Facts and Speculations of Science, George Gamow. Great physicist's fascinating, readable overview of contemporary science: number theory, relativity, fourth dimension, entropy, genes, atomic structure, much more. 128 illustrations. Index. 352pp. 5⅜ × 8½. 25664-2 Pa. $8.95

ENGINEERING IN HISTORY, Richard Shelton Kirby, et al. Broad, nontechnical survey of history's major technological advances: birth of Greek science, industrial revolution, electricity and applied science, 20th-century automation, much more. 181 illustrations. ". . . excellent . . ."—Isis. Bibliography. vii + 530pp. 5⅜ × 8¼.
26412-2 Pa. $14.95

Prices subject to change without notice.

Available at your book dealer or write for free catalog to Dept. GI, Dover Publications, Inc., 31 East 2nd St., Mineola, N.Y. 11501. Dover publishes more than 500 books each year on science, elementary and advanced mathematics, biology, music, art, literary history, social sciences and other areas.